essential
onions

essential
onions

over 80 delicious recipes using onions, leeks, garlic, shallots, scallions and chives

brian glover

southwater

This edition is published by Southwater

Southwater is an imprint of Anness Publishing Ltd
Hermes House, 88–89 Blackfriars Road, London SE1 8HA
tel. 020 7401 2077; fax 020 7633 9499
www.southwaterbooks.com; info@anness.com

© Anness Publishing Ltd 2002

This edition distributed in the UK by The Manning Partnership Ltd
tel. 01225 478 444; fax 01225 478 440
sales@manning-partnership.co.uk

This edition distributed in Australia by Pan Macmillan Australia
tel. 1300 135 113; fax 1300 135 103
email customer.service@macmillan.com.au

This edition distributed in the USA and Canada by
National Book Network
tel. 301 459 3366; fax 301 459 1705
www.nbnbooks.com

This edition distributed in New Zealand by
The Five Mile Press (NZ) Ltd
tel. (09) 444 4144; fax (09) 444 4518
fivemilenz@clear.net.nz

A CIP catalogue record for this book is available from the British Library.

Publisher: Joanna Lorenz
Managing Editor: Linda Fraser
Project Editor: Jennifer Schofield
Designers: Isobel Gillan and Nigel Partridge
Jacket Design: Balley Design Associates
Photographer: William Lingwood
Food for Photography: Sunil Vijayakar (recipes) and Tonia Hedley (reference)
Stylist: Helen Trent

Previously published as part of a larger compendium, *Onion*

1 3 5 7 9 10 8 6 4 2

NOTES
Bracketed terms are intended for American readers.

For all recipes, quantities are given in both metric and imperial measures and, where
appropriate, measures are also given in standard cups and spoons.
Follow one set, but not a mixture, because they are not interchangeable.

Standard spoon and cup measures are level.
1 tsp = 5ml, 1 tbsp = 15ml, 1 cup = 250ml/8fl oz

Australian standard tablespoons are 20ml. Australian readers should use 3 tsp in place of
1 tbsp for measuring small quantities of gelatine, flour, salt, etc.

Medium (US large) eggs are used unless otherwise stated.

Contents

KNOW YOUR ONIONS

To describe onions as essential is entirely appropriate. Where would we be without these wonderfully aromatic vegetables? With other members of the allium family – shallots, leeks, spring onions (scallions) and chives – they flavour all manner of dishes, from soups and salads to stir-fries and hearty stews. There can be scarcely a savoury recipe that doesn't include alliums in some form or other. Their contribution can be subtle and understated, as when chopped chives are used in a potato pancake, or they can make a bolder, more strident statement, like the shallots and garlic that are the central ingredients of a savoury tarte tatin.

Onions and their culinary cousins are inexpensive, easy to store and immensely versatile. They can be eaten raw or cooked, and, even in relatively small quantities, give excellent returns in terms of flavour and health benefits.

Below: The variety of onions available is on the increase, providing a wide range of colours, sizes, flavours and pungency.

HEALTH AND NUTRITION

Although all alliums have been credited with conferring health benefits, garlic is regarded as being particularly useful in reducing blood pressure, helping to lower LDL (low-density lipo-protein) cholesterol and possibly even reducing the build-up of cholesterol within the arteries. Raw garlic has long been considered an effective antibiotic. It may not be so powerful as modern antibiotics, but the way it works is so different that it can kill strains of bacteria that have become antibiotic resistant. Garlic and onions also have considerable antifungal and antiviral properties. Links have been made between garlic and cancer prevention, and experts agree that even a small amount every day will help to strengthen the immune system.

Onions contain vitamins B and C, together with calcium, iron and potassium. Like garlic, they are also a source of cycloallin, an anticoagulant that helps protect against some kinds of heart disease.

ALL THE ALLIUMS

The time when you could send someone to the stores with a shopping list that simply read "onions" is long gone. Today there are liable to be many different types of onion available, as well as all the other alliums.

ONION VARIETIES

Yellow onions are the most common type. Characterized by light brown skin and greenish white to pale yellow flesh, these include the large mild Spanish or Bermuda onions, the sweet Vidalia onions from the United States and the more pungent French onions. These onions are suitable for most culinary purposes and the large ones are especially good stuffed.

Red onions tend to be mild and sweet. Their shiny, papery skins are a glorious purple-red, and this colour can also be glimpsed at the edges of the layers inside. Use red onions raw in salsas, relishes, antipasti and salads. They are also excellent roasted.

White onions tend to be medium to large in size, with papery white skin and white flesh. They are generally quite strongly flavoured.

Cipolla onions, also known as borettane onions, are small and squat, with pale golden skin and yellow flesh, sometimes tinged with pink. They have a sweet flavour and an agreeable depth of taste. Use them whole if possible. Cipolla onions are very good caramelized.

Pickling onions This term is used fairly loosely to describe onions that are particularly small, either because they have been bred that way or because they are immature. Apart from their obvious use in pickles, they can be substituted for shallots in stews and similar dishes. There are yellow and red varieties, as well as the tiny white silverskin pickling onions.

Grelots are small green-skinned onions with very white flesh. Flattish in shape, they resemble bulbous spring onions (scallions) and are often labelled salad onions. Grelots have a mild flavour with a crisp bite, and taste great in salads, stir-fries and omelettes.

SHALLOTS

Unlike onions, shallots grow in clusters or bunches. Most are smaller than onions and have finer layers. They also contain less water and have a more concentrated flavour than onions. There are several varieties, ranging from mild banana shallots to pungent, but not harsh, pink shallots or *èchalote grise* from France. Brown shallots, which are sometimes labelled English or Dutch shallots, are small, with tan skins which often enclose several subsidiary bulbs. Good all-rounders, they are quite mild in flavour. Shallots are good roasted whole, caramelized or pickled. Cooked shallots are used in sauces that require the flavour of onion without the bulk.

LEEKS

Although there are many hundreds of varieties of cultivated leek, they vary only in size and winter hardiness. In recent years, baby leeks have increased in popularity, and while these may simply be immature standard winter leeks, there are now special varieties that are grown to mature quickly and provide slender, tender leaves throughout the summer. Young leeks can be used raw in salads, but the vegetable is usually steamed, braised or blanched and grilled (broiled).

SPRING ONIONS

Most of what are sold as spring or salad onions (scallions in the United States) are simply early-maturing varieties of the onion known as *Allium cepa*. They range in size from pencil-thin specimens to vegetables that are about the size of a baby leek. Spring onions have a mild, sweet flavour with a fresh green snap, which makes them good in salads, salsas and stir-fries.

GARLIC

Love it or loathe it, garlic is one allium it is impossible to ignore. Even a small amount will add immeasurably to the flavour of a dish. There are many different varieties, some with very white skin; others mottled deep pink. Elephant garlic is a particularly large type, with a mild, creamy flavour.

Above: Large leeks, with their sweet, mild flavour, are among the most popular of alliums in the modern kitchen. They are excellent in soups and cooked salads.

Although redolent of garlic, it is actually more closely related to the leek.

If you come across heads of garlic that are tan-brown in colour, they have probably been hot-smoked. This process gives the garlic a deliciously different flavour. Smoked garlic tastes good in garlic butter or mayonnaise.

A typical bulb, or head, of garlic consists of several separate cloves, each wrapped in its own papery skin, but there is also a variety in which each small bulb comprises a single clove. Prepare garlic according to the depth of flavour required: thinly sliced is milder than chopped garlic, which in turn is milder than crushed garlic. For the mildest flavour of all, roast heads of garlic whole. The flesh will become sweet, mellow and so soft and creamy that the purée can simply be popped out of the individual cloves. It is important not to let garlic burn when you are cooking it or it will taste bitter.

In spring and early summer, keep an eye open for the new-season garlic. Unlike dried garlic, which has only limited moisture, new-season garlic is juicy and it tastes mild and sweet.

Above: There are many different kinds of garlic, which are often geographically specific: white garlic is popular in California. California Late and Silverskin are well-known varieties.

OTHER ALLIUMS

Bunching onions are also known as Welsh onions, *chiboules* or *cibols*. Like shallots, they grow in clusters of bulbs, which can be harvested separately. Bunching onions are particularly popular in China and Japan, where their mild flavour is enjoyed in stir-fries and other similar dishes.

Tree onions are vigorous, clumping onions that grow well in the herb patch. Like bunching onions, they grow in such a way that individual bulbs can be removed as needed.

Chives are classified as alliums, although they are most often thought of as herbs. European chives grow well in pots, and the first shoots are often remarkably pungent. Chinese chives, which are also known as garlic chives or *kuchai* (*gow choy* in Cantonese), are even more strongly flavoured and are usually cooked. Chives are very often used as a garnish, and also add flavour to egg and cheese dishes. If you stir chopped chives into an egg or dairy mixture, you must use it quickly, or the chives will tend to taint the other ingredients in the mixture.

PREPARING ONIONS AND OTHER ALLIUMS

CHOPPING ONIONS

1 Peel the onion by cutting off the top and bottom, slit the skin with a sharp knife and peel it off. Slice the peeled onion in half from top to bottom. Lay it cut side down on the chopping board and slice across the onion, leaving a small section uncut at the root end.

2 Slice down through the onion at right angles to these cuts from neck to root. Leave the root end uncut as this will prevent the onion from falling apart, making the next step easier.

3 Finally, slice across the onion at right angles to the second set of cuts. The onion will now fall neatly into dice on the chopping board as you cut.

SLICING ONIONS

1 Cut a peeled onion in half from its neck to root. Place each half in turn cut side down. Hold the onion firmly and slice down with a sharp knife. Be careful to keep your fingers out of the way of the blade.

CUTTING ONION RINGS

1 To achieve perfectly round rings, choose evenly shaped onions. Cut a thin slice from one side of the onion, to provide a steady surface on which it can rest.

2 Stand the onion upright so that it rests on the flat area, and, using a sharp knife, cut into slices. Push the slices out to separate into rings.

SLICING LEEKS

1 Having trimmed and washed the leek, cut it across into thick or thin slices as needed. For stir-frying, cut diagonal slices to present a larger surface area to the heat, ensuring that it cooks quickly.

CHOPPING LEEKS

1 Using a sharp knife, carefully cut the leek in half vertically from top to root, and wash it thoroughly. Lay it cut side down and make a series of cuts along its length, leaving the root end intact so that it doesn't fall apart.

2 Holding the root end firmly, cut across the leek and it will fall neatly into dice on the chopping board.

PEELING GARLIC

1 The easiest way to peel garlic is to place the clove on a chopping board and lay the blade of a cook's knife flat on top. Press down firmly on the blade with the heel of your hand to break the skin of the garlic. This will bruise the garlic, enhancing the flavour.

2 Working from the top of the clove towards the root end, peel off and discard the papery skin.

3 If you have a lot of garlic to peel, it is easier to do this by blanching it first. Cut off the top and bottom of each clove. Place in a bowl of boiling water for 2–3 minutes. Drain, then slip the cloves out of their skins.

CHOPPING GARLIC

1 When chopping or crushing garlic, you may need to remove a green shoot from the centre of one or more cloves. Shoots are most apparent in late winter or early spring and can taste bitter. Pinch them out or cut them out with a knife tip.

2 The finer you chop or crush garlic, the stronger the flavour will be. For a mild flavour, cut it into thin slices across the clove, or chop coarsely.

3 If a stronger flavour is required, finely chop the garlic by first cutting the clove in half from top to bottom, then cutting along and finally cut across the clove.

CRUSHING GARLIC

1 To extract the maximum flavour from garlic, the cloves should be crushed. Chop the garlic coarsely, sprinkle it with flakes of coarse salt, then use the flat side of a broad-bladed knife to work it to a paste.

PREPARING SPRING ONIONS/SCALLIONS

1 Cut the roots off the spring onions, and remove any tough or damaged green leaves. Peel away the thin, outer layer from the stem. For serving the onions whole, trim the leaves neatly.

2 For slices, cut off any coarse green tops, hold several stems together and cut straight down or on the diagonal of the spring onions.

COOKING ONIONS AND OTHER ALLIUMS

FRYING ONIONS

1 Heat whatever oil a recipe calls for in a large, heavy frying pan. Add the chopped or sliced onions. Cook over a medium heat for about 5 minutes until they begin to turn brown at the edges. Stir frequently and do not let them burn. For slow frying, cook over a very low heat for 10–15 minutes.

2 If a recipe calls for onions to be sweated, fry them over a very low heat, but cover the pan with a lid to produce a much softer, sweeter result.

3 To sweat onions even more intensely, press a round of baking parchment over them before covering the onions with the lid.

CARAMELIZING ONIONS

1 Cook onions slowly in butter or oil until they soften. Stir frequently.

2 When the onions begin to brown at the edges, sprinkle over 2.5–5ml/ ½–1 tsp sugar and continue to cook, stirring constantly, until they are golden and caramelized.

CARAMELIZING ONIONS IN THE OVEN

1 Place thickly sliced onions in a roasting pan, season well and sprinkle with chopped herbs. Drizzle with a little oil and cover with foil. Bake at 190°C/375°F/Gas 5 for 30 minutes, then remove the foil, stir in 5ml/1 tsp sugar and drizzle with a little balsamic vinegar. Bake for a further 35 minutes.

PREPARING ONIONS FOR STUFFING

1 Choose round, even-shaped onions. Peel, but leave the top and especially the root base intact.

2 Blanch the onions by cooking in a pan of lightly salted, boiling water for approximately 15 minutes. Drain well and set aside until cool enough to handle. Cut off and remove a cap from the top of each onion.

3 Using a small, sharp knife and a pointed or serrated teaspoon, remove the centre of the onion to leave a shell 2–3 layers thick. Fill with your chosen stuffing and brush with a little oil or butter. Bake in a preheated oven at 180°C/350°F/Gas 4 for 45–60 minutes.

VICHYSSOISE

THIS CLASSIC CHILLED SUMMER SOUP WAS FIRST CREATED IN THE 1920S BY LOUIS DIAT, CHEF AT THE NEW YORK RITZ-CARLTON. HE NAMED IT AFTER VICHY NEAR HIS HOME IN FRANCE. IT IS BASED ON A SIMPLE LEEK AND POTATO SOUP, MADE LUXURIOUSLY VELVETY BY ADDING CREAM.

3 Stir in the stock or water, 5ml/1 tsp salt and pepper to taste. Bring to the boil, then reduce the heat and partly cover the pan. Simmer for 15 minutes, or until the potatoes are soft.

4 Cool, then process the soup until smooth in a blender or food processor. Sieve the soup into a bowl and stir in the cream. Taste and adjust the seasoning and add a little iced water if the consistency of the soup seems too thick.

5 Chill the soup for at least 4 hours, or until very cold. Taste the chilled soup for seasoning and add a squeeze of lemon juice, if required. Pour the soup into bowls and sprinkle with chopped chives. Serve immediately.

VARIATIONS
• **Potage Bonne Femme** For this hot leek and potato soup, use 1 chopped onion instead of the shallots and 450g/1lb potatoes. Halve the quantity of double (heavy) cream and reheat it in the puréed soup, adding a little milk if the consistency of the soup seems very thick. Deep-fried shredded leek may be used to garnish the soup instead of chives.
• **Chilled Leek and Sorrel or Watercress Soup** Add about 50g/2oz/1 cup shredded sorrel to the soup at the end of cooking. Finish and chill as in the main recipe, then serve the soup garnished with a little pile of finely shredded sorrel. The same quantity of watercress can be used in the same way.

SERVES FOUR TO SIX

INGREDIENTS
 50g/2oz/¼ cup unsalted
  (sweet) butter
 450g/1lb leeks, white parts only,
  thinly sliced
 3 large shallots, sliced
 250g/9oz floury potatoes (such as
  King Edward or Maris Piper), peeled
  and cut into small chunks
 1 litre/1¾ pints/4 cups light chicken
  stock or water
 300ml/½ pint/1¼ cups double
  (heavy) cream
 iced water (optional)
 a little lemon juice (optional)
 salt and ground black pepper
 chopped fresh chives, to garnish

1 Melt the butter in a heavy pan and cook the leeks and shallots gently, covered, for 15–20 minutes, until soft but not browned.

2 Add the potatoes to the pan and cook, uncovered, for a few minutes.

SHERRIED ONION AND ALMOND SOUP WITH SAFFRON

THE SPANISH COMBINATION OF ONIONS, SHERRY AND SAFFRON GIVES THIS PALE YELLOW SOUP A BEGUILING FLAVOUR THAT IS PERFECT FOR THE OPENING COURSE OF A SPECIAL MEAL.

2 Add the saffron strands and cook, uncovered, for 3–4 minutes, then add the ground almonds and cook, stirring constantly, for another 2–3 minutes. Pour in the stock and sherry and stir in 5ml/1 tsp salt. Season with plenty of black pepper. Bring to the boil, then lower the heat and simmer gently for about 10 minutes.

SERVES FOUR

INGREDIENTS
40g/1½oz/3 tbsp butter
2 large yellow onions, thinly sliced
1 small garlic clove, finely chopped
generous pinch of saffron threads
  (about 12 threads)
50g/2oz/½ cup finely ground, toasted
  blanched almonds
750ml/1¼ pints/3 cups good chicken
  or vegetable stock
45ml/3 tbsp dry sherry
salt and ground black pepper
30ml/2 tbsp flaked (sliced) or
  slivered almonds, toasted, and
  chopped fresh parsley to garnish

1 Melt the butter in a heavy pan over a low heat. Add the onions and garlic, stirring to coat them thoroughly in the butter, then cover the pan and cook very gently, stirring frequently, for 15–20 minutes, until the onions are soft and golden yellow.

VARIATION
This soup is also delicious served chilled. Use olive oil rather than butter and add a little more chicken or vegetable stock to make a slightly thinner soup, then leave to cool and chill for at least 4 hours. Just before serving, taste for seasoning. Float 1–2 ice cubes in each bowl.

3 Process the soup in a blender or food processor until smooth, then return it to the rinsed pan. Reheat slowly, without allowing the soup to boil, stirring occasionally. Taste for seasoning, adding more salt and pepper if required.

4 Ladle the soup into heated bowls, garnish with the toasted flaked or slivered almonds and a little parsley and serve immediately.

SIMPLE CREAM OF ONION SOUP

THIS WONDERFULLY SOOTHING SOUP HAS A DEEP, BUTTERY FLAVOUR THAT IS COMPLEMENTED BY CRISP CROÛTONS OR CHOPPED CHIVES, SPRINKLED OVER JUST BEFORE SERVING.

SERVES FOUR

INGREDIENTS
  115g/4oz/½ cup unsalted
    (sweet) butter
  1kg/2¼lb yellow onions, sliced
  1 fresh bay leaf
  105ml/7 tbsp dry white vermouth
  1 litre/1¾ pints/4 cups good chicken
    or vegetable stock
  150ml/¼ pint/⅔ cup double
    (heavy) cream
  a little lemon juice (optional)
  salt and ground black pepper
  croûtons or chopped fresh chives,
    to garnish

COOK'S TIP
Adding the second batch of onions gives texture and a buttery flavour to this soup.

1 Melt 75g/3oz/6 tbsp of the butter in a large, heavy pan. Set about 200g/7oz of the onions aside and add the rest to the pan with the bay leaf. Stir to coat in the butter, then cover and cook over a very low heat for about 30 minutes. The onions should be very soft and tender, but not browned.

2 Add the vermouth, increase the heat and boil rapidly until the liquid has evaporated. Add the stock, 5ml/1 tsp salt and pepper to taste. Bring to the boil, lower the heat and simmer for 5 minutes, then remove from the heat.

3 Leave the soup to cool, then discard the bay leaf and process it in a blender or food processor. Return the soup to the rinsed pan.

4 Meanwhile, melt the remaining butter in another pan and cook the remaining onions slowly, covered, until soft but not browned. Uncover and continue to cook gently until golden yellow.

5 Add the cream to the soup and reheat it gently until hot, but do not allow it to boil. Taste and adjust the seasoning, adding a little lemon juice if you like. Add the buttery onions and stir for 1–2 minutes, then ladle the soup into bowls. Sprinkle with croûtons or chopped chives and serve.

CHICKEN, LEEK AND CELERY SOUP

THIS MAKES A SUBSTANTIAL MAIN COURSE SOUP WITH FRESH CRUSTY BREAD. YOU WILL NEED NOTHING MORE THAN A SALAD AND CHEESE, OR JUST FRESH FRUIT TO FOLLOW.

SERVES FOUR TO SIX

INGREDIENTS
1.4kg/3lb chicken
1 small head of celery, trimmed
1 onion, coarsely chopped
1 fresh bay leaf
a few fresh parsley stalks
a few fresh tarragon sprigs
2.4 litres/4 pints/10 cups cold water
3 large leeks
65g/2½oz/5 tbsp butter
2 potatoes, cut into chunks
150ml/¼ pint/⅔ cup dry white wine
30–45ml/2–3 tbsp single (light)
  cream (optional)
salt and ground black pepper
90g/3½oz pancetta, grilled (broiled)
  until crisp, to garnish

1 Cut the breast portions off the chicken and set aside. Chop the rest of the chicken carcass into 8–10 pieces and place in a large pan.

2 Chop 4–5 of the outer sticks of the celery and add them to the pan with the onion. Tie the bay leaf, parsley and tarragon together and add to the pan. Pour in the cold water to cover the ingredients and bring to the boil. Reduce the heat and cover the pan, then simmer for 1½ hours.

3 Remove the chicken and cut off and reserve the meat. Strain the stock, then return it to the pan and boil rapidly until it has reduced to about 1.5 litres/ 2½ pints/6¼ cups.

4 Meanwhile, set about 150g/5oz of the leeks aside. Slice the remaining leeks and the remaining celery, reserving any celery leaves. Chop the celery leaves and set aside to garnish the soup.

5 Melt half the butter in a large, heavy pan. Add the sliced leeks and celery, cover and cook over a low heat for about 10 minutes, or until softened but not browned. Add the potatoes, wine and 1.2 litres/2 pints/5 cups of the chicken stock.

6 Season well with salt and pepper, bring to the boil and reduce the heat. Part-cover the pan and simmer the soup for 15–20 minutes, or until the potatoes are cooked.

7 Meanwhile, skin the reserved chicken breast portions and cut the flesh into pieces. Melt the remaining butter in a frying pan, add the chicken and cook for 5–7 minutes, until tender.

8 Thickly slice the remaining leeks, add to the pan and cook, stirring occasionally, for a further 3–4 minutes, until just cooked.

9 Process the soup with the cooked chicken from the stock in a blender or food processor. Taste and adjust the seasoning, and add more stock if the soup is very thick.

10 Stir in the cream, if using, and the chicken and leek mixture. Reheat the soup gently. Serve in warmed bowls. Crumble the pancetta over the soup and sprinkle with the chopped celery leaves.

LITTLE ONIONS COOKED <u>WITH</u> WINE, CORIANDER <u>AND</u> OLIVE OIL

IF YOU CAN FIND THE SMALL, FLAT ITALIAN CIPOLLA OR BORETTANE ONIONS, THEY ARE EXCELLENT IN THIS RECIPE — OTHERWISE USE PICKLING ONIONS, SMALL RED ONIONS OR SHALLOTS.

3 Add the currants, reduce the heat and cook gently for 15–20 minutes, or until the onions are tender but not falling apart. Use a slotted spoon to transfer the onions to a serving dish.

4 Boil the liquid over a high heat until it reduces considerably. Taste and adjust the seasoning, if necessary, then pour the reduced liquid over the onions. Sprinkle the oregano over the onions, set aside to cool and then chill them.

5 Just before serving, stir in the grated lemon rind, chopped parsley and toasted pine nuts.

SERVES SIX

INGREDIENTS
    105ml/7 tbsp olive oil
    675g/1½lb small onions, peeled
    150ml/¼ pint/⅔ cup dry white wine
    2 bay leaves
    2 garlic cloves, bruised
    1–2 small dried red chillies
    15ml/1 tbsp lightly crushed, toasted
      coriander seeds
    2.5ml/½ tsp sugar
    a few fresh thyme sprigs
    30ml/2 tbsp currants
    10ml/2 tsp chopped fresh oregano
    5ml/1 tsp grated lemon rind
    15ml/1 tbsp chopped fresh flat
      leaf parsley
    30–45ml/2–3 tbsp pine nuts, toasted
    salt and ground black pepper

1 Place 30ml/2 tbsp olive oil in a wide pan. Add the onions and cook gently over a medium heat for about 5 minutes, or until they begin to colour. Remove from the pan and set aside.

2 Add the remaining oil, the wine, bay leaves, garlic, chillies, coriander, sugar and thyme to the pan. Bring to the boil and cook briskly for 5 minutes. Return the onions to the pan.

COOK'S TIP
Serve this dish as one of several small dishes – an antipasto – perhaps with mustard mayonnaise-dressed celeriac salad and some thinly sliced prosciutto or other air-dried ham.

GRILLED SPRING ONIONS AND ASPARAGUS WITH PROSCIUTTO

THIS IS A GOOD CHOICE OF FIRST COURSE AT THE BEGINNING OF SUMMER, WHEN BOTH SPRING ONIONS AND ASPARAGUS ARE AT THEIR BEST. THE SLIGHT SMOKINESS OF THE GRILLED VEGETABLES GOES VERY WELL WITH THE SWEETNESS OF THE AIR-DRIED HAM.

SERVES FOUR TO SIX

INGREDIENTS

    2 bunches of plump spring onions
      (scallions) (about 24)
    500g/1¼lb asparagus
    45–60ml/3–4 tbsp olive oil
    20ml/4 tsp balsamic vinegar
    8–12 slices prosciutto
    50g/2oz pecorino cheese
    sea salt and ground black pepper
    extra virgin olive oil,
      to serve

COOK'S TIP
The spring onions (scallions) can be cooked on a ridged griddle pan. If more convenient, the asparagus can be roasted at 200°C/400°F/Gas 6 for 15 minutes.

1 Trim the root, outer papery skin and the top off the spring onions.

2 Cut off and discard the woody ends of the asparagus and use a vegetable peeler to peel the lower 7.5cm/3in of the spears.

3 Heat the grill (broiler). Toss the spring onions and asparagus in 30ml/2 tbsp of the oil. Place on two baking sheets and season.

4 Grill (broil) the asparagus for about 5 minutes on each side, until just tender when tested with the tip of a sharp knife. Protect the tips with foil if necessary. Grill the spring onions for 3–4 minutes on each side, until tinged with brown. Brush both vegetables with more oil when you turn them.

5 Arrange the vegetables on plates. Season with pepper and drizzle with vinegar. Lay 2–3 slices of ham on each plate and shave over the pecorino. Serve extra virgin olive oil for drizzling.

LEEK TERRINE WITH RED PEPPERS

THIS PRESSED LEEK TERRINE LOOKS VERY PRETTY WHEN SLICED AND SERVED ON INDIVIDUAL PLATES WITH THE DRESSING DRIZZLED OVER AND AROUND THE SLICES.

SERVES SIX TO EIGHT

INGREDIENTS
- 1.8kg/4lb slender leeks
- 4 large red (bell) peppers, halved and seeded
- 15ml/1 tbsp extra virgin olive oil
- 10ml/2 tsp balsamic vinegar
- 5ml/1 tsp ground toasted cumin seeds
- salt and ground black pepper

For the dressing
- 120ml/4fl oz/½ cup extra virgin olive oil
- 1 garlic clove, bruised and peeled
- 5ml/1 tsp Dijon mustard
- 5ml/1 tsp soy sauce
- 15ml/1 tbsp balsamic vinegar
- pinch of caster (superfine) sugar
- 2.5–5ml/½–1 tsp ground toasted cumin seeds
- 15–30ml/1–2 tbsp chopped mixed fresh basil and flat leaf parsley

COOK'S TIP
It is easier to slice the terrine if you leave the clear film (plastic wrap) on and use a very sharp knife or an electric carving knife. Transfer the slices to the plates, then remove the clear film.

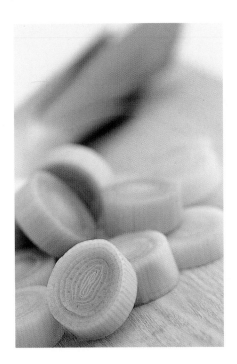

1 Line a 23cm/9in-long terrine or loaf tin (pan) with clear film (plastic wrap), leaving the ends overhanging. Cut the leeks to the same length as the tin.

2 Cook the leeks in salted, boiling water for 5–7 minutes, until just tender. Drain thoroughly and leave to cool, then squeeze out as much water as possible from the leeks and leave them to drain on a clean dishtowel.

3 Grill (broil) the red peppers, skin side uppermost, until the skin blisters and blackens. Place in a bowl, cover and leave for 10 minutes. Peel the peppers and cut the flesh into long strips, then place them in a bowl and add the oil, balsamic vinegar and ground toasted cumin. Season to taste with salt and pepper and toss well.

4 Layer the leeks and strips of red pepper in the lined tin, alternating the layers so that the white of the leeks in one row is covered by the green of the next row. Season the leeks with a little more salt and pepper.

5 Cover with the overhanging clear film. Top with a plate and weigh it down with heavy food cans or weights. Chill for several hours or overnight.

6 To make the dressing, place the oil, garlic, mustard, soy sauce and vinegar in a jug (pitcher) and mix thoroughly. Season and add the sugar. Add ground cumin to taste and leave to stand for several hours. Discard the garlic and add the fresh herbs to the dressing.

7 Unmould the terrine and cut it into thick slices. Put 1–2 slices on each plate, drizzle with dressing and serve.

ROAST GARLIC <u>WITH</u> GOAT'S CHEESE, WALNUT <u>AND</u> HERB PÂTÉ

THE COMBINATION OF SWEET, MELLOW ROASTED GARLIC AND GOAT'S CHEESE IS A CLASSIC ONE. THIS IS PARTICULARLY GOOD MADE WITH THE NEW SEASON'S WALNUTS, SOMETIMES KNOWN AS "WET" WALNUTS, WHICH ARE AVAILABLE IN THE EARLY AUTUMN.

SERVES FOUR

INGREDIENTS
    4 large heads of garlic
    4 fresh rosemary sprigs
    8 fresh thyme sprigs
    60ml/4 tbsp olive oil
    sea salt and ground black pepper
For the pâté
    200g/7oz soft goat's cheese
    5ml/1 tsp finely chopped fresh thyme
    15ml/1 tbsp chopped fresh parsley
    50g/2oz/½ cup walnuts, chopped
    15ml/1 tbsp walnut oil (optional)
    fresh thyme, to garnish
To serve
    4–8 slices sourdough bread
    shelled walnuts

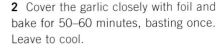

1 Preheat the oven to 180°C/350°F/ Gas 4. Strip the skin from the heads of garlic. Place them in an ovenproof dish large enough to hold them snugly. Tuck in the rosemary and thyme, drizzle the oil over and season to taste.

2 Cover the garlic closely with foil and bake for 50–60 minutes, basting once. Leave to cool.

3 Preheat the grill (broiler). To make the pâté, cream the cheese with the thyme, parsley and chopped walnuts. Beat in 15ml/1 tbsp of the cooking oil from the garlic and season to taste, then transfer the pâté to a serving bowl.

4 Brush the sourdough bread with the remaining cooking oil from the garlic, then grill (broil) until toasted.

5 Drizzle the walnut oil, if using, over the goat's cheese pâté and grind some black pepper over it. Place a bulb of garlic on each plate and serve with the pâté and some of the toasted bread. Garnish with a little fresh thyme and serve a few freshly shelled walnuts and a little sea salt with each portion.

TAPENADE WITH QUAIL'S EGGS AND CRUDITÉS

TAPENADE MAKES A SOCIABLE START TO A MEAL. SERVE WITH HARD-BOILED QUAIL'S EGGS AND VEGETABLE CRUDITÉS AND LET EVERYONE HELP THEMSELVES.

SERVES SIX

INGREDIENTS
   225g/8oz/2 cups pitted black olives
   2 large garlic cloves, peeled
   15ml/1 tbsp salted capers, rinsed
   6 canned or bottled anchovy
     fillets, drained
   50g/2oz good-quality canned tuna
   5–10ml/1–2 tsp Cognac (optional)
   5ml/1 tsp chopped fresh thyme
   30ml/2 tbsp chopped fresh parsley
   30–60ml/2–4 tbsp extra virgin
     olive oil
   a dash of lemon juice
   30ml/2 tbsp crème fraîche or sour
     cream (optional)
   12–18 quail's eggs
   ground black pepper
For the crudités
   bunch of spring onions (scallions),
     halved if large
   bunch of radishes, trimmed
   bunch of baby fennel, trimmed and
     halved if large, or 1 large fennel
     bulb, cut into thin wedges
To serve
   French bread
   unsalted (sweet) butter
   sea salt

1 Process the olives, garlic, capers, anchovies and tuna in a food processor or blender. Blend in the Cognac, if using, the thyme, parsley and enough olive oil to make a paste. Season to taste with pepper and a dash of lemon juice. Stir in the crème fraîche or sour cream, if using, and transfer the tapenade to a serving bowl.

2 Place the quail's eggs in a pan, cover with cold water and bring to the boil. Cook for only 2 minutes, then immediately drain and plunge the eggs into iced water to stop them from cooking further and to make them easier to shell.

3 When the eggs are cold, carefully part-shell them.

4 Arrange the tapenade with the eggs and crudités and serve, offering French bread, unsalted butter and sea salt to accompany them.

COOK'S TIPS
• Crème fraîche or sour cream softens the flavour of the olives for a milder tapenade.
• In Provence, where tapenade comes from, it is traditional to serve it with crudités of celery, fennel and tomato.
• Tapenade is also delicious spread on thin slices of toasted French bread and served as an appetizer with pre-dinner drinks. It may be garnished with chopped hard-boiled egg.

GUACAMOLE

THIS DISH HAS ALMOST BECOME A CLICHÉ OF TEX-MEX COOKING, USUALLY SERVED AS A FIRST COURSE WITH BREAD OR CORN CHIPS FOR DIPPING. CAREFULLY SEASONED, IT IS A GREAT ACCOMPANIMENT FOR SIMPLE GRILLED FISH, POULTRY OR MEAT, ESPECIALLY STEAK.

SERVES FOUR

INGREDIENTS

2 large ripe avocados
1 small red onion, very
    finely chopped
1 red or green chilli, seeded and very
    finely chopped
½–1 garlic clove, crushed with a
    little salt (optional)
finely shredded rind of ½ lime and
    juice of 1–1½ limes
pinch of caster (superfine) sugar
225g/8oz tomatoes, seeded
    and chopped
30ml/2 tbsp coarsely chopped fresh
    coriander (cilantro)
2.5–5ml/½–1 tsp ground toasted
    cumin seeds
15ml/1 tbsp olive oil
15–30ml/1–2 tbsp sour
    cream (optional)
salt and ground black pepper
lime wedges, dipped in sea salt, and
    fresh coriander sprigs, to garnish

1 Halve, stone (pit) and peel the avocados. Set one half aside and mash the remainder in a bowl using a fork.

COOK'S TIP
Leaving some of the avocado in chunks adds a slightly different texture, but if you prefer, mash all the avocado together. Hard avocados will soften in a few seconds in a microwave. Check frequently until you get the degree of softness you like.

2 Add the onion, chilli, garlic (if using), lime rind, juice of 1 lime, sugar, tomatoes and coriander. Add ground cumin, seasoning and more lime juice to taste. Stir in the olive oil.

3 Dice the remaining avocado and stir into the guacamole, then cover and leave to stand for 15 minutes so that the flavour develops. Stir in the sour cream, if using. Serve immediately with lime wedges, dipped in sea salt, and coriander sprigs.

BAGNA CAUDA

This hot garlic dip from Piedmont in northern Italy is outrageously rich as it contains olive oil, butter and cream. Literally translated, the name means "a hot bath", and in Piedmont it is traditionally eaten to celebrate the end of the grape harvest.

SERVES FOUR

INGREDIENTS

   150ml/¼ pint/⅔ cup extra virgin
     olive oil
   5cm/2in fresh rosemary sprig
   6 garlic cloves, thinly sliced or
     finely chopped
   50g/2oz can anchovy fillets, drained
     and chopped
   90g/3½oz/7 tbsp unsalted
     (sweet) butter
   75ml/5 tbsp double (heavy) cream
   ground black pepper
To serve
   a selection of vegetables, such as
     new potatoes, baby artichokes,
     cauliflower florets, and baby carrots
   crusty bread
   large cooked prawns (shrimp)

1 Prepare the serving ingredients you have chosen for dipping according to type. Cook them if necessary – new potatoes and baby artichokes, for example – and cut the bread and large vegetables into small portions.

VARIATIONS
• In Piedmont, they sometimes add a little very finely shaved white truffle. Add this at the very end to appreciate the wonderful aroma of the truffle.
• The rosemary is not traditional, but the slight bitterness it imparts cuts the rich sauce. Omit it if you prefer.
• Omit the cream for a stronger-tasting, less rich dip, and use a light olive oil from Provence or Liguria instead.

2 Place the olive oil in a small pan over a very low heat, then add the fresh rosemary and sliced or chopped garlic. Keep the heat low for about 5 minutes so that the flavour of the garlic permeates the oil, but do not allow the garlic to brown.

3 Add the anchovies, remove the rosemary and cook for 3–5 minutes, mashing the anchovies into the oil with a wooden spoon. Keep the heat low to make sure the garlic does not brown.

4 When the anchovies have broken down completely, add the butter and cream and whisk gently until the butter has melted. Season to taste with a little pepper.

5 Pour the mixture into a fondue pan or small earthenware container and stand this over a spirit stove or nightlight to keep the bagna cauda warm. Surround with the bread, vegetables and prawns for dipping and serve immediately.

CHICKEN LIVER PÂTÉ <u>WITH</u> GARLIC

THIS SMOOTH, GARLICKY PÂTÉ IS WICKEDLY INDULGENT BUT ABSOLUTELY DELICIOUS. IT IS IDEAL AS A FIRST COURSE, WITH TOAST AND SOME SMALL PICKLED GHERKINS OR CORNICHONS. IT IS ALSO GOOD WITH CONFIT OF SLOW-COOKED ONIONS.

SERVES SIX TO EIGHT

INGREDIENTS
  225g/8oz/1 cup unsalted
    (sweet) butter
  400g/14oz chicken livers, chopped
  45–60ml/3–4 tbsp Madeira
  3 large shallots, chopped
  2 large garlic cloves, finely chopped
  5ml/1 tsp finely chopped fresh thyme
  pinch of ground allspice
  30ml/2 tbsp double (heavy)
    cream (optional)
  salt and ground black pepper
  small fresh bay leaves or fresh thyme
    sprigs, to garnish

VARIATION
Use duck livers instead of chicken and add 2.5ml/½ tsp grated orange rind.

1 Melt 75g/3oz/6 tbsp butter in a small pan over a low heat, then leave it to bubble gently until it is clear. Pour off the clarified butter into a bowl.

2 Melt 40g/1½oz/3 tbsp butter in a frying pan and fry the chicken livers for 4–5 minutes, until browned.

3 Add the Madeira and set it alight, then scrape the contents of the pan into a food processor or blender.

4 Melt 25g/1oz/2 tbsp butter in the pan over a low heat and cook the shallots for 5 minutes, until soft. Add the garlic, thyme and allspice and cook for a further 2–3 minutes. Add this mixture to the livers with the remaining butter and cream, if using, then process until smooth.

5 Add about 7.5ml/1½ tsp each of salt and pepper and more Madeira to taste. Scrape the pâté into a serving dish and place a few bay leaves or thyme sprigs on top. Melt the clarified butter, if necessary, then pour it over the pâté. Cool and chill for 4 hours or overnight.

COOK'S TIP
The flavour of the pâté deepens and matures on chilling, so it is best if you make it a day before it is required.

STILTON-STUFFED MUSHROOMS BAKED IN GARLIC BREADCRUMBS

SERVE THESE SUCCULENT STUFFED MUSHROOMS WITH CHUNKS OF WARM, CRUSTY BREAD OR FRESH ROLLS TO SOAK UP ALL THEIR DELICIOUS GARLIC-FLAVOURED JUICES.

SERVES FOUR

INGREDIENTS

    450g/1lb chestnut mushrooms
    3 garlic cloves, finely chopped
    90g/3½oz/7 tbsp butter, melted
    juice of ½ lemon
    115g/4oz Stilton cheese, crumbled
    50g/2oz/½ cup walnuts, chopped
    90g/3½oz/1½ cups fresh
      white breadcrumbs
    25g/1oz/⅓ cup freshly grated
      Parmesan cheese
    30ml/2 tbsp chopped fresh parsley
    salt and ground black pepper

COOK'S TIP
A simple sauce of thick Greek (US strained plain) yogurt with some chopped fresh herbs and a little Dijon mustard stirred through goes well with these Stilton-stuffed mushrooms.

1 Preheat the oven to 200°C/400°F/ Gas 6. Place the mushrooms in an ovenproof dish and sprinkle half the garlic over them. Drizzle with 60ml/ 4 tbsp of the butter and the lemon juice. Season with salt and pepper and bake for 15–20 minutes. Leave to cool.

2 Cream the crumbled Stilton with the chopped walnuts and mix in 30ml/ 2 tbsp of the breadcrumbs.

3 Divide the Stilton mixture among the mushrooms.

4 Preheat the grill (broiler). Mix the remaining garlic, breadcrumbs and melted butter together. Stir in the Parmesan and parsley and season with pepper. Cover the mushrooms with the breadcrumb mixture and grill (broil) for about 5 minutes, or until crisp and browned. Serve immediately.

BAKED EGGS EN COCOTTE
WITH WILD MUSHROOMS AND CHIVES

THESE SIMPLE, BUT UTTERLY DELICIOUS, BAKED EGGS MAKE A SPLENDID START TO A LIGHT MEAL OR AN EXCELLENT DISH FOR BRUNCH. SERVE WITH HOT, BUTTERED TOAST.

SERVES FOUR TO SIX

INGREDIENTS
   65g/2½oz/5 tbsp butter
   2 shallots, finely chopped
   1 small garlic clove, finely chopped
   250g/9oz/3⅔ cups finely chopped
     mixed wild mushrooms
   15ml/1 tbsp lemon juice
   5ml/1 tsp chopped fresh tarragon
   30ml/2 tbsp crème fraîche
   30ml/2 tbsp chopped fresh chives
   4–6 eggs
   salt and ground black pepper
   whole chives, to garnish
   buttered toast, to serve

COOK'S TIP
The eggs may also be cooked by standing the dishes in a covered frying pan containing 2.5cm/1in boiling water. Cook over a medium heat for 8–10 minutes.

1 Melt 50g/2oz/4 tbsp of the butter in a pan over a medium-low heat and cook the shallots and garlic gently, stirring occasionally, for 5 minutes, until softened but not browned.

2 Increase the heat and add the mushrooms, then cook briskly, stirring frequently, until the mushrooms lose their moisture and begin to brown.

3 Stir in the lemon juice and tarragon and continue to cook over a medium heat, stirring occasionally, until the mushrooms absorb the liquid. Stir in half the crème fraîche and half the chopped chives and season to taste.

4 Preheat the oven to 190°C/375°F/ Gas 5. Distribute the mushroom mixture equally among 4–6 large ramekins or small ovenproof dishes of about 150–175ml/5–6fl oz/⅔–¾ cup capacity. Sprinkle the remaining chopped chives over the mushrooms.

5 Break an egg into each dish, add a dash of crème fraîche and season to taste with black pepper. Dot with the remaining butter and bake in the centre of the oven for 10–15 minutes, or until the whites of the eggs are set and the yolks cooked to your liking.

6 Serve immediately, garnished with fresh chives and accompanied by lots of hot, buttered toast.

LEEK, SAFFRON AND MUSSEL TARTS

SERVE THESE VIVIDLY COLOURED LITTLE TARTS AS A FIRST COURSE, WITH A FEW SALAD LEAVES, SUCH AS WATERCRESS, ROCKET AND FRISÉE. ALTERNATIVELY, COOK THE FILLING IN ONE 23CM/9IN TART SHELL AND SERVE IT AS A MAIN COURSE WITH SALAD AND FRESH BREAD.

2 Soak the saffron in the hot water for 10 minutes. Cook the leeks in the oil in a large pan over a medium heat for 6–8 minutes, until softened and beginning to brown. Add the pepper strips and cook for a further 2 minutes.

3 Bring 2.5cm/1in depth of water to a rolling boil in a large pan and add 10ml/2 tsp salt. Discard any open mussels that do not shut when tapped sharply, then throw the rest into the pan. Cover and cook over a high heat, shaking the pan occasionally, for 3–4 minutes, or until the mussels open. Discard any mussels that do not open. Shell the mussels.

SERVES SIX

INGREDIENTS
- 350g/12oz shortcrust pastry, thawed if frozen
- large pinch of saffron threads (about 15 threads)
- 15ml/1 tbsp hot water
- 2 large leeks, sliced
- 30ml/2 tbsp olive oil
- 2 large yellow (bell) peppers, halved, seeded, grilled (broiled) and peeled, then cut into strips
- 900g/2lb fresh mussels, scrubbed and beards removed
- 2 large (US extra large) eggs
- 300ml/½ pint/1¼ cups single (light) cream
- 30ml/2 tbsp finely chopped fresh parsley
- salt and ground black pepper

1 Preheat the oven to 190°C/375°F/Gas 5. Roll out the pastry and use to line 6 × 10cm/4in tartlet tins (muffin pans), 2.5cm/1in deep. Prick the bases and line the sides with foil. Bake for 10 minutes. Remove the foil and bake for 5–8 minutes, until lightly coloured. Remove from the oven. Reduce the temperature to 180°C/350°F/Gas 4.

4 Beat the eggs, cream and saffron liquid together. Season well with salt and pepper and whisk in the parsley.

5 Arrange the leek and yellow pepper mixture and mussels in the pastry cases, add the egg mixture and bake for 20–25 minutes, until risen and just firm. Serve immediately.

RED ONION AND MUSHROOM TARTLETS WITH GOAT'S CHEESE

CRISP AND SAVOURY, THESE ATTRACTIVE LITTLE TARTS ARE DELICIOUS SERVED WITH A FEW MIXED SALAD LEAVES DRIZZLED WITH A GARLIC-FLAVOURED FRENCH DRESSING.

SERVES SIX

INGREDIENTS
    60ml/4 tbsp olive oil
    25g/1oz/2 tbsp butter
    4 red onions, thinly sliced
    5ml/1 tsp brown sugar
    15ml/1 tbsp balsamic vinegar
    15ml/1 tbsp soy sauce
    200g/7oz button (white) mushrooms,
      thinly sliced
    1 garlic clove, finely chopped
    2.5ml/½ tsp chopped fresh tarragon
    30ml/2 tbsp chopped fresh parsley
    250g/9oz goat's cheese
      log (*chèvre*)
    salt and ground black pepper
    mixed salad leaves, to serve
For the pastry
    200g/7oz/1¾ cups plain (all-
      purpose) flour
    pinch of cayenne pepper
    90g/3½oz/7 tbsp butter
    40g/1½oz/½ cup freshly grated
      Parmesan cheese
    45–60ml/3–4 tbsp iced water

1 First make the pastry. Sift the flour and cayenne into a bowl, add the butter, then rub in with the fingertips until the mixture resembles breadcrumbs.

2 Stir in the grated Parmesan, then bind the pastry with the iced water, adding just enough to give a firm dough. Press the pastry together into a ball, wrap in clear film (plastic wrap) and chill for at least 45 minutes.

3 Heat 15ml/1 tbsp of the oil and half the butter in a heavy frying pan, then add the onions, cover and cook gently for 15 minutes, stirring occasionally.

4 Uncover the pan, increase the heat slightly and sprinkle in the brown sugar. Cook, stirring frequently, until the onions begin to caramelize and brown. Add the vinegar and soy sauce and cook briskly until the liquid evaporates. Season to taste then set aside.

5 Heat another 30ml/2 tbsp of the oil and the remaining butter in a pan, then add the mushrooms and garlic and cook over a medium heat for about 5–6 minutes, until the mushrooms are browned and cooked.

6 Set a few mushrooms and onion rings aside, then stir the rest of the mushrooms into the onions with the tarragon and parsley. Adjust the seasoning to taste. Preheat the oven to 190°C/375°F/Gas 5.

7 Roll out the pastry and use to line 6 × 10cm/4in tartlet tins (muffin pans), preferably loose-based and metal. Prick the pastry bases with a fork and line the sides with strips of foil. Bake for 10 minutes, remove the foil and bake for a further 5–7 minutes, or until the pastry is lightly browned and cooked. Remove from the oven and increase the temperature to 200°C/400°F/Gas 6.

8 Remove the pastry cases (pie shells) from the tins and arrange them on a baking sheet. Distribute the onion mixture equally among the pastry cases. Cut the goat's cheese into 6 equal slices and place 1 slice on each tartlet. Add a few reserved mushrooms and onion slices to each tartlet, drizzle with the remaining olive oil and season lightly with pepper.

9 Return the tartlets to the oven and bake for 5–8 minutes, or until the goat's cheese is just beginning to turn brown. Serve with mixed salad leaves.

POTATO AND CHIVE PANCAKES WITH PICKLED HERRING AND ONION RINGS

THESE PANCAKES ARE FULL OF DELICIOUS SCANDINAVIAN FLAVOURS. SERVE THEM AS A FIRST COURSE OR AS A LIGHT MAIN COURSE WITH SALAD. SMALL PANCAKES MAKE EXCELLENT CANAPÉS TO SERVE WITH ICE-COLD SHOTS OF VODKA OR OTHER PRE-DINNER DRINKS.

SERVES SIX

INGREDIENTS
    275g/10oz peeled potatoes
    2 eggs, beaten
    150ml/¼ pint/⅔ cup milk
    40g/1½oz plain (all-purpose) flour
    30ml/2 tbsp chopped fresh chives
    vegetable oil or butter, for greasing
    salt and ground black pepper
For the topping
    2 small red or yellow onions, thinly
        sliced into rings
    60ml/4 tbsp sour cream or
        crème fraîche
    5ml/1 tsp wholegrain mustard
    15ml/1 tbsp chopped fresh dill
    6 pickled herring fillets
To garnish
    fresh dill sprigs
    fresh chives or chive flowers

1 Cut the potatoes into chunks and cook them in salted, boiling water for about 15 minutes, or until tender, then drain and mash or sieve to form a smooth purée.

2 Meanwhile prepare the topping. Place the onions in a bowl and cover with boiling water. Set aside for 2–3 minutes, then drain thoroughly and dry on kitchen paper.

3 Mix the onions with the sour cream or crème fraîche, mustard and chopped dill. Season to taste.

4 Using a sharp knife, cut the pickled herring fillets into 12–18 pieces. Set them aside.

5 Put the potato purée in a bowl and beat in the eggs, milk and flour with a wooden spoon to make a batter. Season to taste with salt and pepper and whisk in the chopped chives.

6 Heat a non-stick frying pan over a medium heat and grease it with a little oil or butter. Spoon about 30ml/2 tbsp of batter into the pan to make a pancake measuring about 7.5cm/3in across. Cook for 3–4 minutes, until the underside is set and golden brown. Turn the pancake over and cook the other side for 3–4 minutes, until golden brown. Transfer to a plate and keep warm while you make the remaining pancakes in batches of 3–4. The mixture will make 12 pancakes.

7 Place two pancakes on each of six warmed plates and distribute the pickled herring fillets and onions equally among them. Garnish with dill sprigs, fresh chives and/or chive flowers. Season with black pepper and serve immediately.

MOUCLADE

THIS IS A TRADITIONAL DISH OF MUSSELS COOKED WITH SHALLOTS, GARLIC AND SAFFRON FROM THE WEST ATLANTIC COAST OF FRANCE. IT TASTES AS SUPERB AS IT LOOKS.

SERVES SIX

INGREDIENTS
2kg/4½lb fresh mussels, scrubbed
   and beards removed
250g/9oz shallots, finely chopped
300ml/½ pint/1¼ cups medium white
   wine, such as Vouvray
generous pinch of saffron threads
   (about 12 threads)
75g/3oz/6 tbsp butter
2 celery sticks, finely chopped
5ml/1 tsp fennel seeds,
   lightly crushed
2 large garlic cloves, finely chopped
250ml/8fl oz/1 cup fish stock
1 bay leaf
pinch of cayenne pepper
2 large (US extra large) egg yolks
150ml/¼ pint/⅔ cup double
   (heavy) cream
juice of ½–1 lemon
30–45ml/2–3 tbsp chopped
   fresh parsley
salt and ground black pepper

1 Discard any mussels that do not shut when tapped sharply.

2 Place 30ml/2 tbsp of the shallots with the wine in a wide pan and bring to the boil. Add half the mussels and cover, then boil rapidly for 1 minute, shaking the pan once. Remove all the mussels, discarding any that remain closed. Repeat with the remaining mussels. Remove the top half-shell from each mussel. Strain the cooking liquid through a fine sieve into a bowl and stir in the saffron, then set aside.

3 Melt 50g/2oz/4 tbsp of the butter in a heavy pan. Add the remaining shallots and celery and cook over a low heat, stirring occasionally, for 5–6 minutes, until softened but not browned. Add the fennel seeds and half of the garlic, then cook for a further 2–3 minutes.

4 Pour in the reserved mussel liquid, bring to the boil and then simmer for 5 minutes before adding the stock, bay leaf and cayenne. Season with salt and pepper to taste, then simmer, uncovered, for 5–10 minutes.

5 Beat the egg yolks with the cream, then whisk in a ladleful of the hot liquid followed by the juice of ½ lemon. Whisk this mixture back into the sauce. Cook over a very low heat, without allowing it to boil, for 5–10 minutes until slightly thickened. Taste for seasoning and add more lemon juice if necessary.

6 Stir the remaining garlic, butter and most of the parsley into the sauce with the mussels and reheat for 30–60 seconds. Distribute the mussels among 6 soup plates and ladle the sauce over. Sprinkle with the remaining parsley and serve.

GRILLED ONION AND AUBERGINE SALAD WITH GARLIC AND TAHINI DRESSING

THIS IS A DELICIOUSLY SMOKY SALAD THAT BALANCES SWEET AND SHARP FLAVOURS. IT MAKES A GOOD FILLING FOR PITTA BREAD, WITH SOME CRISP LETTUCE AND SWEET, RIPE TOMATOES.

SERVES SIX

INGREDIENTS
    3 aubergines (eggplants), cut into
      1cm/½in thick slices
    675g/1½lb round, not flat, onions,
      thickly sliced
    75–90ml/5–6 tbsp olive oil
    5ml/1 tsp powdered sumac (optional)
    45ml/3 tbsp coarsely chopped flat
      leaf parsley
    45ml/3 tbsp pine nuts, toasted
    salt and ground black pepper
For the dressing
    2 garlic cloves, crushed
    150ml/¼ pint/⅔ cup light tahini
    juice of 1–2 lemons
    45–60ml/3–4 tbsp water

1 Place the aubergines on a rack or in a colander and sprinkle generously with salt. Leave for 45–60 minutes, then rinse thoroughly under cold running water and pat dry with kitchen paper.

2 Thread the onions on to skewers or place them in an oiled hinged rack.

COOK'S TIPS
• Sumac is a Mediterranean spice with a sharp, lemony taste. Buy it ready ground at Middle Eastern stores, good wholefood stores or delicatessens.
• Tahini is a thick, smooth, oily paste made from sesame seeds. It is also available from Middle Eastern stores, wholefood stores and delicatessens and from some supermarkets.

3 Brush the aubergines and onions with about 45ml/3 tbsp of the oil and grill (broil) for 6–8 minutes on each side. Brush with more oil, if necessary, when you turn the vegetables. The vegetables should be browned and soft when cooked. The onions may need a little longer than the aubergines.

4 Arrange the vegetables on a serving dish and sprinkle with the sumac, if using, and season with salt and pepper to taste. Sprinkle with the remaining oil if they seem dry.

5 For the dressing, crush the garlic with a pinch of salt in a mortar and gradually work in the tahini. Gradually work in the juice of 1 lemon, followed by the water. Taste and add more lemon juice if you think the dressing needs it. Thin with more water, if necessary, so that the dressing is fairly runny.

6 Drizzle the dressing over the salad and leave for 30–60 minutes, then sprinkle with the chopped parsley and pine nuts. Serve immediately at room temperature, not chilled.

BEETROOT AND RED ONION SALAD

THIS SALAD LOOKS ESPECIALLY ATTRACTIVE WHEN MADE WITH A MIXTURE OF RED AND YELLOW BEETROOT. TRY IT WITH ROAST BEEF OR COOKED HAM AS IT TASTES EXCELLENT WITH THESE RICH MEATS.

SERVES SIX

INGREDIENTS
    500g/1¼lb small beetroot (beets)
    75ml/5 tbsp water
    60ml/4 tbsp olive oil
    90g/3½oz/scant 1 cup walnut or
        pecan halves
    5ml/1 tsp caster (superfine) sugar,
        plus a little extra for the dressing
    30ml/2 tbsp walnut oil
    15ml/1 tbsp sherry vinegar or
        balsamic vinegar
    5ml/1 tsp soy sauce
    5ml/1 tsp grated orange rind
    2.5ml/½ tsp ground roasted
        coriander seeds
    5–10ml/1–2 tsp orange juice
    1 red onion, halved and very
        thinly sliced
    15–30ml/1–2 tbsp chopped
        fresh fennel
    75g/3oz watercress or
        mizuna leaves
    handful of baby red chard or
        beetroot leaves (optional)
    salt and ground black pepper

3 Meanwhile, heat 15ml/1 tbsp of the olive oil in a small frying pan and cook the walnuts or pecans until they begin to brown. Add the sugar and cook, stirring, until the nuts begin to caramelize. Season with 2.5ml/½ tsp salt and lots of pepper, then turn the nuts out on to a plate and leave to cool.

4 In a jug (pitcher) or bowl, whisk together the remaining olive oil, the walnut oil, sherry or balsamic vinegar, soy sauce, orange rind and ground roasted coriander to make the dressing. Season with salt and pepper to taste and add a pinch of caster sugar. Whisk in orange juice to taste.

5 Separate the red onion slices into half-rings and add them to the strips of beetroot. Add the dressing and toss thoroughly to mix.

6 When ready to serve, toss the salad with the fennel, watercress or mizuna and red chard or beetroot leaves, if using. Transfer to individual bowls or plates and sprinkle with the caramelized nuts. Serve immediately.

1 Preheat the oven to 180°C/350°F/Gas 4. Place the beetroot in an ovenproof dish just large enough to hold them in a single layer and add the water. Cover tightly and cook in the oven for about 1–1½ hours, or until they are just tender.

2 Cool, then peel the beetroot, then slice them or cut them into strips and toss with 15ml/1 tbsp of the olive oil. Transfer to a bowl and set aside.

LEEK SALAD WITH ANCHOVIES, EGGS AND PARSLEY

CHOPPED HARD-BOILED EGGS AND COOKED LEEKS ARE A CLASSIC COMBINATION IN FRENCH-STYLE SALADS. THIS ONE MAKES A GOOD FIRST COURSE, WITH SOME CRUSTY BREAD, OR A LIGHT MAIN DISH THAT CAN BE FINISHED WITH A TOMATO SALAD AND/OR A POTATO SALAD.

3 To make the dressing, whisk the mustard with the vinegar. Gradually whisk in the oil, followed by the cream. Stir in the shallot, then season to taste with salt, pepper and a pinch of caster sugar, if you like.

4 Leave the leeks whole or thickly slice them, then place in a serving dish. Pour most of the dressing over them and stir to mix. Leave for at least 1 hour, or until ready to serve, bringing them back to room temperature first, if necessary.

5 Arrange the anchovies on the leeks, then sprinkle the eggs and parsley over the top. Drizzle with the remaining dressing, season with black pepper and dot with a few olives, if using. Serve immediately.

SERVES FOUR

INGREDIENTS
  675g/1½lb thin or baby
    leeks, trimmed
  2 large (US extra large) or 3 medium
    (US large) eggs
  50g/2oz good-quality anchovy
    fillets in olive oil, drained
  15g/½oz flat leaf parsley, chopped
  a few black olives, pitted (optional)
  salt and ground black pepper
For the dressing
  5ml/1 tsp Dijon mustard
  15ml/1 tbsp tarragon vinegar
  75ml/5 tbsp olive oil
  30ml/2 tbsp double
    (heavy) cream
  1 small shallot, very
    finely chopped
  pinch of caster sugar (optional)

1 Cook the leeks in salted, boiling water for 3–4 minutes. Drain, plunge into cold water, then drain again. Squeeze out excess water, then pat dry.

2 Place the eggs in a pan of cold water, bring to the boil and cook for 6–7 minutes. Drain, plunge into cold water, then shell and chop the eggs.

COOK'S TIP
Make sure the leeks are well drained and squeezed of excess water or they will dilute the dressing and spoil the flavour.

PARSLEY AND ROCKET SALAD WITH BLACK OLIVE AND GARLIC DRESSING

BEING LIGHT BUT FULL OF FLAVOUR, THIS MAKES A WELL-ROUNDED FIRST COURSE; IT IS ALSO GOOD SERVED ALONGSIDE RARE ROAST BEEF. USE THE BEST PARMESAN CHEESE — PARMIGIANO REGGIANO — TO MAKE SURE THAT THIS SALAD IS SPECIAL.

SERVES SIX

INGREDIENTS
  1 garlic clove, halved
  115g/4oz good white bread, cut into
    1cm/½in thick slices
  45ml/3 tbsp olive oil, plus extra for
    shallow frying
  75g/3oz rocket (arugula) leaves
  75g/3oz baby spinach
  25g/1oz flat leaf parsley, leaves only
  45ml/3 tbsp salted capers, rinsed
    and dried
  40g/1½oz Parmesan cheese, pared
    into shavings
For the dressing
  25ml/5 tsp black olive paste
  1 garlic clove, finely chopped
  5ml/1 tsp Dijon mustard
  75ml/5 tbsp olive oil
  10ml/2 tsp balsamic vinegar
  ground black pepper

1 First make the dressing. Whisk the black olive paste, garlic and mustard together in a bowl. Gradually whisk in the olive oil, then the vinegar. Adjust the seasoning with black pepper – the dressing should be sufficiently salty.

2 Heat the oven to 190°C/375°F/Gas 5. Rub the halved garlic clove over the bread and cut or tear the slices into bitesize croûtons. Toss them in the oil and place on a small baking tray. Bake for 10–15 minutes, stirring once, until golden brown. Cool on kitchen paper.

3 Mix the rocket, spinach and parsley in a large salad bowl.

4 Heat a shallow layer of olive oil in a frying pan. Add the capers and cook until crisp. Scoop out immediately and drain on kitchen paper.

5 Toss the dressing and croûtons into the salad and divide it among six bowls or plates. Sprinkle the Parmesan shavings and the crisp capers over the top and serve immediately.

COOK'S TIP
Use a swivel-action or fixed-blade potato peeler to cut thin shavings from a block of Parmigiano Reggiano. It is easier to make shavings if you choose a relatively young cheese rather than an older, drier and much harder Parmesan. Alternatively some supermarkets sell tubs of ready-shaved cheese.

MOROCCAN ORANGE, ONION AND OLIVE SALAD

THIS IS A REFRESHING SALAD TO FOLLOW A RICH MAIN DISH, SUCH AS A MOROCCAN TAGINE OF LAMB, OR TO LIGHTEN ANY SPICY MEAL. IT IS ALSO DELICIOUS WITH COLD ROAST DUCK.

SERVES SIX

INGREDIENTS
    5 large oranges
    90g/3½oz/scant 1 cup black olives
    1 red onion, thinly sliced
    1 large fennel bulb, thinly sliced,
        feathery tops reserved
    15ml/1 tbsp chopped fresh mint,
        plus a few extra sprigs
    15ml/1 tbsp chopped fresh coriander
        (cilantro), plus a few extra sprigs
    2.5ml/½ tsp orange flower water
For the dressing
    60ml/4 tbsp olive oil
    10ml/2 tsp lemon juice
    2.5ml/½ tsp ground toasted
        coriander seeds
    salt and ground black pepper

1 Peel the oranges with a sharp knife, making sure you remove all the white pith, and cut them into 5mm/¼in slices. Remove any pips (seeds) and work over a bowl to catch all the orange juice. Set the juice aside.

2 Pit the olives, if you like. In a bowl, toss the orange slices, onion and fennel together with the olives, chopped mint and fresh coriander.

3 Make the dressing. In a bowl or jug (pitcher), whisk together the olive oil, 15ml/1 tbsp of the reserved fresh orange juice and the lemon juice. Add the ground toasted coriander seeds and season to taste with a little salt and pepper. Whisk thoroughly to mix.

4 Toss the dressing into the salad and leave to stand for 30–60 minutes.

5 Drain off any excess dressing and place the salad on a serving dish. Sprinkle with the herbs and fennel tops, and the orange flower water.

TOMATO, MOZZARELLA AND RED ONION SALAD WITH BASIL AND CAPER DRESSING

SWEET TOMATOES AND THE HEADY SCENT OF BASIL CAPTURE THE ESSENCE OF SUMMER IN THIS SIMPLE SALAD. VINE-RIPENED TOMATOES USUALLY HAVE THE BEST FLAVOUR.

SERVES FOUR

INGREDIENTS
    5 large ripe tomatoes, peeled if
        you like
    2 buffalo mozzarella cheeses,
        drained and sliced
    1 small red onion, chopped
For the dressing
    ½ small garlic clove, peeled
    15g/½oz fresh basil
    30ml/2 tbsp chopped fresh flat
        leaf parsley
    25ml/5 tsp salted capers, rinsed
    2.5ml/½ tsp mustard
    75–90ml/5–6 tbsp extra virgin
        olive oil
    5–10ml/1–2 tsp balsamic vinegar
    salt and ground black pepper
For the garnish
    fresh basil leaves
    fresh parsley sprigs

1 First make the dressing. Put the garlic, basil, parsley, half the capers and the mustard in a food processor or blender and process briefly to chop. Then, with the motor running, gradually pour in the olive oil through the feeder tube to make a smooth purée with a dressing consistency. Add the balsamic vinegar to taste and season with ground black pepper.

2 Slice the tomatoes. Arrange the tomato and mozzarella slices on a plate. Sprinkle the onion over and season with a little pepper.

3 Drizzle the dressing over the salad, then sprinkle a few basil leaves, parsley sprigs and the remaining capers on top as a garnish. Leave for 10–15 minutes before serving.

LEEK AND GRILLED RED PEPPER SALAD WITH GOAT'S CHEESE

THE CONTRASTING TEXTURES OF SILKY, GRILLED PEPPERS, SOFT CHEESE AND SLIGHTLY CRISP LEEKS MAKES THIS SALAD EXTRA-SPECIALLY DELICIOUS. THIS MAKES A GOOD FIRST COURSE SERVED WITH CRUSTY BREAD.

3 Halve and seed the peppers, then grill (broil) them, skin side uppermost, until the skin is blackened and blistered. Place them in a bowl, cover and leave to stand for 10 minutes, so that they soften in their own steam. Remove the skin and cut the flesh into strips, then mix with the leeks and thyme, adding pepper to taste.

4 Make the dressing by shaking all the ingredients together in a jar, adding seasoning to taste. Pour the dressing over the salad and chill it for several hours. Bring the salad back to room temperature before serving.

SERVES SIX

INGREDIENTS
  4 × 1cm/½in thick slices French
    goat's cheese log (*chèvre*)
  65g/2½oz/1 cup fine dry
    white breadcrumbs
  675g/1½lb young slender
    leeks, trimmed
  15ml/1 tbsp olive oil
  2 large red (bell) peppers
  few fresh thyme sprigs, chopped
  vegetable oil, for shallow frying
  45ml/3 tbsp chopped fresh flat
    leaf parsley
  salt and ground black pepper
For the dressing
  75ml/5 tbsp extra virgin olive oil
  1 small garlic clove, finely chopped
  5ml/1 tsp Dijon mustard, plain or
    flavoured with herbes de Provence
  15ml/1 tbsp red wine vinegar

1 Remove any skin from the cheese and roll the slices in the breadcrumbs, pressing them in so that the cheese is well coated. Chill the cheese for 1 hour.

2 Cook the leeks in salted, boiling water for 3–4 minutes. Drain and cut into 7.5–10cm/3–4in lengths. Toss in the oil and season. Grill (broil) the leeks for 3–4 minutes on each side.

5 When ready to serve, heat a shallow layer of vegetable oil in a large, non-stick frying pan and cook the goat's cheeses quickly until golden brown on each side. Drain them well on kitchen paper and cool slightly, then cut into bitesize pieces. Toss the cheese and chopped parsley into the salad and serve immediately.

LENTIL AND SPINACH SALAD WITH ONION, CUMIN AND GARLIC

THIS WONDERFUL, EARTHY SALAD IS GREAT FOR A PICNIC OR WITH BARBECUED FOOD. IT IMPROVES WITH STANDING AND IS AT ITS BEST SERVED AT ROOM TEMPERATURE RATHER THAN CHILLED.

SERVES SIX

INGREDIENTS
225g/8oz/1 cup Puy lentils
1 fresh bay leaf
1 celery stick
fresh thyme sprig
30ml/2 tbsp olive oil
1 onion or 3–4 shallots,
  finely chopped
10ml/2 tsp crushed toasted
  cumin seeds
400g/14oz young spinach
salt and ground black pepper
30–45ml/2–3 tbsp chopped fresh
  parsley, plus a few extra sprigs
For the dressing
75ml/5 tbsp extra virgin olive oil
5ml/1 tsp Dijon mustard
15–25ml/3–5 tsp red wine vinegar
1 small garlic clove, finely chopped
2.5ml/½ tsp finely grated lemon rind

1 Rinse the lentils thoroughly and place them in a large pan. Add plenty of water to cover. Tie the bay leaf, celery and thyme into a bundle and add to the pan, then bring to the boil. Reduce the heat so that the water boils steadily. Cook the lentils for 30–45 minutes, until just tender.

2 Meanwhile, to make the dressing, mix the oil, mustard, 15ml/3 tsp vinegar, the garlic and lemon rind, and season well with salt and pepper.

3 Thoroughly drain the lentils and turn them into a bowl. Add most of the dressing and toss well, then set the lentils aside, stirring occasionally.

COOK'S TIP
Originally grown around the town of Puy in south-west France, these grey-green lentils have an excellent, earthy flavour and keep their shape on cooking. Do not add salt when cooking as it toughens the outer skin. Season when cooked.

4 Heat the oil in a deep frying pan and cook the onion or shallots over a low heat for about 4–5 minutes, until they are beginning to soften. Add the cumin and cook for 1 minute.

5 Add the spinach and season to taste, cover and cook for 2 minutes. Stir, then cook again briefly until wilted.

6 Stir the spinach into the lentils and leave the salad to cool. Bring back to room temperature if necessary. Stir in the remaining dressing and chopped parsley. Adjust the seasoning, adding extra red wine vinegar if necessary.

7 Turn the salad on to a serving platter and sprinkle over some parsley sprigs.

THAI PRAWN SALAD WITH GARLIC DRESSING AND FRIZZLED SHALLOTS

IN THIS INTENSELY FLAVOURED SALAD, SWEET PRAWNS AND MANGO ARE PARTNERED WITH A SWEET-SOUR GARLIC DRESSING HEIGHTENED WITH THE HOT TASTE OF CHILLI. THE CRISP FRIZZLED SHALLOTS ARE A TRADITIONAL ADDITION TO THAI SALADS.

SERVES FOUR TO SIX

INGREDIENTS
675g/1½lb raw prawns (shrimp),
  shelled and deveined with tails on
finely shredded rind of 1 lime
½ fresh red chilli, seeded and
  finely chopped
30ml/2 tbsp olive oil, plus extra
  for brushing
1 ripe but firm mango
2 carrots, cut into long thin shreds
10cm/4in piece cucumber, sliced
1 small red onion, halved and
  thinly sliced
a few fresh coriander (cilantro) sprigs
a few fresh mint sprigs
45ml/3 tbsp roasted peanuts,
  coarsely chopped
4 large shallots, thinly sliced and
  fried until crisp in 30ml/2 tbsp
  groundnut (peanut) oil
salt and ground black pepper
For the dressing
1 large garlic clove, chopped
10–15ml/2–3 tsp caster (superfine)
  sugar
juice of 2 limes
15–30ml/1–2 tbsp Thai fish sauce
1 red chilli, seeded
5–10ml/1–2 tsp light rice vinegar

1 Place the prawns in a glass or china dish and add the lime rind and chilli. Season with salt and pepper and spoon the oil over them. Toss to mix and leave to marinate for 30–40 minutes.

2 For the dressing, place the garlic in a mortar with 10ml/2 tsp caster sugar and pound until smooth, then work in the juice of 1½ limes and 15ml/1 tbsp of the Thai fish sauce.

3 Transfer the dressing to a jug (pitcher). Finely chop half the chilli. and add it to the dressing. Taste and add more sugar, lime juice, fish sauce and the rice vinegar to taste.

COOK'S TIP
To devein prawns (shrimp), make a shallow cut down the back of the prawn using a small, sharp knife. Using the tip of the knife, lift out the thin, black vein, then rinse the prawn thoroughly under cold, running water.

4 Peel and stone (pit) the mango, then cut it into very fine strips.

5 Toss together the mango, carrots, cucumber and onion and half the dressing. Arrange the salad on individual plates or in bowls.

6 Heat a ridged, cast-iron griddle pan or heavy frying pan until very hot. Brush with a little oil, then sear the prawns for 2–3 minutes on each side, until they turn pink and are patched with brown on the outside. Arrange the prawns on the salads.

7 Sprinkle the remaining dressing over the salads and sprinkle the sprigs of coriander and mint over. Finely shred the remaining chilli and sprinkle it over the salads with the peanuts and crisp-fried shallots. Serve immediately.

WARM POTATO SALAD <u>WITH</u> BACON <u>AND</u> SHALLOT DRESSING

THIS WARM SALAD MAKES A FINE ACCOMPANIMENT FOR GRILLED SAUSAGES OR SMOKED MACKEREL.
TARRAGON VINEGAR AND MUSTARD WITH TARRAGON OR FINES HERBES ARE GOOD IN THE DRESSING.

SERVES SIX

INGREDIENTS
900g/2lb salad potatoes (waxy variety)
90ml/6 tbsp olive oil
200g/7oz dry-cure streaky (fatty)
  bacon, cut into strips
3 shallots, chopped
1 small garlic clove, finely chopped
30ml/2 tbsp white wine vinegar
30ml/2 tbsp dry white vermouth or
  white wine
5ml/1 tsp French mustard
45–60ml/3–4 tbsp chopped fresh
  herbs, such as chervil, parsley
  and tarragon
15ml/1 tbsp chopped fresh chives
salt and ground black pepper
whole fresh chives, to garnish

1 Cook the potatoes in salted, boiling water for 15–20 minutes, until tender. Drain, cool a little, then peel. Slice the potatoes directly into a bowl and add 45ml/3 tbsp of the oil. Season with pepper to taste. Stir to coat the potatoes, then set aside.

2 Heat a further 30ml/2 tbsp of the oil in a frying pan. Cook the bacon until crisp and lightly browned, then add the shallots and cook, stirring constantly, for 2–3 minutes. Add the garlic and cook for 1 minute. Scrape the contents of the pan over the potatoes and stir to mix.

3 Return the pan to the heat. Add the vinegar and vermouth or wine and reduce a little, then stir in the mustard. Immediately pour this mixture over the potatoes. Add most of the mixed herbs and stir to mix.

4 Spoon the salad into a large serving bowl or individual bowls. Drizzle the remaining oil over the top and sprinkle with the remaining herbs and the chives. Garnish with whole chives, then serve immediately.

JERUSALEM ARTICHOKES WITH GARLIC, SHALLOTS AND BACON

THE SLIGHTLY SMOKY AND EARTHY FLAVOUR OF JERUSALEM ARTICHOKES IS EXCELLENT WITH SHALLOTS AND SMOKED BACON. THESE ARE GOOD WITH CHICKEN, ROAST COD OR MONKFISH, OR PORK.

3 Season with salt and black pepper to taste and stir in the water. Cover and cook for a further 8–10 minutes, shaking the pan occasionally.

4 Uncover the pan, increase the heat and cook for 5–6 minutes, until all the moisture has evaporated and the artichokes are tender.

5 In another frying pan, melt the remaining butter in the olive oil. Add the white breadcrumbs and cook over a medium heat, stirring frequently, until crisp and golden. Stir in the chopped parsley and the reserved cooked bacon or pancetta.

6 Combine the artichokes with the breadcrumb mixture, mixing well. Adjust the seasoning, if necessary, then turn into a warmed serving dish. Serve immediately.

SERVES FOUR

INGREDIENTS
50g/2oz/¼ cup butter
115g/4oz smoked bacon or pancetta, chopped
800g/1¾lb Jerusalem artichokes, peeled
8–12 garlic cloves, peeled
115g/4oz shallots, chopped
75ml/5 tbsp water
30ml/2 tbsp olive oil
25g/1oz/½ cup fresh white breadcrumbs
30–45ml/2–3 tbsp chopped fresh parsley
salt and ground black pepper

1 Melt half the butter in a heavy frying pan and cook the chopped bacon or pancetta until brown and beginning to crisp. Remove half the bacon or pancetta from the pan and set aside.

2 Add the artichokes, garlic and shallots, and cook, stirring frequently, until the artichokes and garlic begin to brown slightly.

COOK'S TIP
Do not peel the artichokes too far in advance as they discolour quickly on exposure to air. If necessary, drop them into a bowl of acidulated water.

BRAISED LETTUCE AND PEAS WITH SPRING ONIONS AND MINT

THIS IS BASED ON THE TRADITIONAL FRENCH WAY OF BRAISING PEAS WITH LETTUCE AND SPRING ONIONS IN BUTTER. IT IS DELICIOUS WITH SIMPLY COOKED FISH OR ROAST OR GRILLED DUCK.

SERVES FOUR

INGREDIENTS

50g/2oz/¼ cup butter
4 Little Gem (Bibb) lettuces, halved lengthways
2 bunches of spring onions (scallions), trimmed
5ml/1 tsp caster (superfine) sugar
400g/14oz/3½ cups shelled peas (about 1kg/2¼lb in pods)
4 fresh mint sprigs
120ml/4fl oz/½ cup chicken stock
15ml/1 tbsp chopped fresh mint
salt and ground black pepper

1 Melt half the butter in a wide, heavy pan over a low heat. Add the lettuces and spring onions.

2 Turn the vegetables in the butter, then sprinkle in the sugar, 2.5ml/½ tsp salt and plenty of black pepper. Cover, and cook very gently for 5 minutes, stirring once.

3 Add the peas and mint sprigs. Turn the peas in the buttery juices and pour in the stock, then cover and cook over a gentle heat for a further 5 minutes. Uncover and increase the heat to reduce the liquid to a few tablespoons.

4 Stir in the remaining butter and adjust the seasoning. Transfer to a warmed serving dish and sprinkle with the chopped mint. Serve immediately.

VARIATIONS
• Braise about 250g/9oz baby carrots with the lettuce.
• Use 1 lettuce, shredding it coarsely, and omit the mint. Towards the end of cooking, stir in about 150g/5oz rocket (arugula), preferably the stronger-flavoured, wild rocket, and cook briefly until wilted.
• Cook 115g/4oz chopped smoked bacon or pancetta with 1 small chopped onion in the butter. Use 1 bunch of spring onions (scallions) and omit the mint. Stir in some chopped parsley before serving. This version is also very good with small summer turnips, braised with the lettuce.

ROASTED SWEET POTATOES, ONIONS AND BEETROOT IN COCONUT AND GINGER PASTE

SWEET POTATOES AND BEETROOT TAKE ON A WONDERFUL SWEETNESS WHEN ROASTED, AND THEY ARE DELICIOUS WITH THE SAVOURY ONIONS AND AROMATIC COCONUT, GINGER AND GARLIC PASTE.

SERVES FOUR

INGREDIENTS
30ml/2 tbsp groundnut (peanut) oil
450g/1lb sweet potatoes, peeled and
   cut into thick strips or chunks
4 beetroot (beets), cooked, peeled
   and cut into wedges
450g/1lb small red or yellow
   onions, halved
5ml/1 tsp coriander seeds,
   lightly crushed
3–4 small whole fresh red chillies
salt and ground black pepper
chopped fresh coriander (cilantro),
   to garnish
For the paste
2 large garlic cloves, chopped
1–2 fresh green chillies, seeded
   and chopped
15ml/1 tbsp chopped fresh
   root ginger
45ml/3 tbsp chopped fresh coriander
75ml/5 tbsp coconut milk
30ml/2 tbsp groundnut oil
grated rind of ½ lime
2.5ml/½ tsp light muscovado
   (brown) sugar

1 First make the paste. Process the garlic, chillies, ginger, coriander and coconut milk in a food processor, blender or coffee grinder.

2 Turn the paste into a small bowl and beat in the oil, lime rind and muscovado sugar. Preheat the oven to 200°C/400°F/Gas 6.

3 Heat the oil in a roasting pan in the oven for 5 minutes. Add the sweet potatoes, beetroot, onions and coriander seeds, tossing them in the hot oil. Roast for 10 minutes.

4 Stir in the paste and the whole red chillies. Season well with salt and pepper, and toss the vegetables to coat them thoroughly with the paste.

5 Roast the vegetables for a further 25–35 minutes, or until the sweet potatoes and onions are fully cooked and tender. Stir 2–3 times to prevent the paste from sticking to the pan. Serve immediately, sprinkled with a little chopped fresh coriander.

COOK'S TIP
Orange-fleshed sweet potatoes look more attractive than white-fleshed ones in this dish – and they are more nutritious.

SWEET-SOUR ROASTED ONIONS

THESE ONIONS ARE DELICIOUS WITH ROAST PORK OR LAMB OR SERVED WITH A CRACKED WHEAT PILAFF.

SERVES FOUR

INGREDIENTS
    4 large onions
    60ml/4 tbsp olive oil
    10ml/2 tsp crushed coriander seeds
    15ml/1 tbsp clear honey
    30ml/2 tbsp pomegranate molasses
    15ml/1 tbsp sherry vinegar
    salt and ground black pepper

COOK'S TIP
Pomegranate molasses is made by boiling down the juice of the fruit to produce a thick, sticky liquid with a wonderful sweet-sour taste. It is available from Middle Eastern food stores and some large supermarkets. There is no suitable substitute.

1 Cut the onions into wedges, leaving them attached at the root end. Preheat the oven to 200°C/400°F/Gas 6. Place the onion wedges, olive oil and crushed coriander in a roasting pan and mix thoroughly with your hands. Season to taste, then roast for 20 minutes.

2 Mix the honey, pomegranate molasses and vinegar with 15ml/1 tbsp water. Drizzle this mixture over the onions and stir to mix. Reduce the oven temperature to 180°C/350°F/Gas 4 and cook for a further 20–30 minutes, until well browned. Serve immediately.

ROASTED RED ONIONS WITH CRUMBLY CHEESE AND SUN-DRIED TOMATO BUTTER

ONIONS ROAST TO A WONDERFUL SWEET CREAMINESS WHEN COOKED IN THEIR SKINS. THEY NEED BUTTER, LOTS OF BLACK PEPPER AND SALTY FOOD TO SET OFF THEIR SWEETNESS.

SERVES SIX

INGREDIENTS
    6 even-sized red onions, unpeeled
    175–225g/6–8oz crumbly cheese
        (such as Lancashire, Caerphilly or
        Cheshire), thinly sliced
    a few chopped fresh chives
    salt and ground black pepper
For the sun-dried tomato butter
    115g/4oz/½ cup butter, softened
    65g/2½oz sun-dried tomatoes in olive
        oil, drained and finely chopped
    30ml/2 tbsp chopped fresh basil
        or parsley

VARIATIONS
• Use goat's cheese instead of Lancashire, Caerphilly or Cheshire.
• Cook fresh white breadcrumbs in butter with a little garlic until crisp and then mix with lots of chopped fresh parsley. Sprinkle the crisp crumb mixture over the onions before serving.

1 Preheat the oven to 180°C/350°F/Gas 4. Put the unpeeled onions in a roasting pan and roast for 1¼–1½ hours, until they are tender and feel soft when lightly squeezed.

2 Meanwhile, prepare the sun-dried tomato butter. Cream the butter and then beat in the tomatoes and basil or parsley. Season to taste with salt and pepper and shape into a roll, then wrap in foil and chill.

3 Slit the tops of the onions and open them up. Season with plenty of black pepper and add chunks of the sun-dried tomato butter. Sprinkle the cheese and chives over the top and eat immediately, mashing the butter and cheese into the soft, sweet onion.

COOK'S TIP
Sun-dried tomatoes are easiest to chop if you snip them into tiny pieces with a sharp pair of kitchen scissors.

CARAMELIZED ONION AND WALNUT SCONES

THESE SCONES ARE VERY GOOD BUTTERED AND SERVED WITH MATURE CHEDDAR OR LANCASHIRE CHEESE. THEY ARE ALSO EXCELLENT WITH SOUP OR A ROBUST VEGETABLE STEW. MAKE SMALL SCONES TO USE AS A BASE FOR COCKTAIL SAVOURIES, SERVED TOPPED WITH A LITTLE SOFT GOAT'S CHEESE.

4 Add the cooked onion, walnuts and fresh thyme, then bind to make a soft, but not sticky, dough with the buttermilk or smetana.

5 Roll or pat out the mixture to just over 1cm/½in thick. Stamp out scones using a 5–6cm/2–2½in round cutter.

MAKES TEN TO TWELVE

90g/3½oz/7 tbsp butter
15ml/1 tbsp olive oil
1 Spanish (Bermuda) onion, chopped
2.5ml/½ tsp cumin seeds, lightly crushed, plus a few extra
200g/7oz/1¾ cups self-raising (self-rising) flour
5ml/1 tsp baking powder
25g/1oz/¼ cup oatmeal
5ml/1 tsp light muscovado (brown) sugar
90g/3½oz/scant 1 cup chopped walnuts
5ml/1 tsp chopped fresh thyme
120–150ml/4–5fl oz/½–⅔ cup buttermilk or smetana
a little milk
salt and ground black pepper
coarse sea salt

1 Melt 15g/½oz/1 tbsp of the butter with the oil and gently cook the onion, covered, for 12 minutes. Uncover and cook gently until it begins to brown.

2 Add the crushed cumin seeds and increase the temperature slightly. Cook, stirring occasionally, until the onion browns and begins to caramelize around the edges. Cool. Preheat the oven to 200°C/400°F/Gas 6.

3 Sift the flour, baking powder and oatmeal into a large bowl and add 2.5ml/½ tsp salt, a generous grinding of black pepper and the muscovado sugar. Add the remaining butter and rub in with the fingertips until the mixture resembles breadcrumbs.

6 Place the scones on a floured baking tray, glaze with milk and sprinkle with a little salt and a few extra cumin seeds. Bake for 12–15 minutes, until well-risen and golden brown. Cool for a few minutes on a wire rack and serve warm.

RED ONION AND ROSEMARY FOCACCIA

THIS BREAD IS RICH IN OLIVE OIL AND IT HAS AN AROMATIC TOPPING OF RED ONION, FRESH ROSEMARY (DRIED ROSEMARY IS NOT SUITABLE) AND CRUNCHY SEA SALT. IT IS GOOD WITH TOMATO OR PEPPER SALADS, OR AS AN ACCOMPANIMENT TO ALL KINDS OF MEDITERRANEAN DISHES.

SERVES FOUR TO FIVE

450g/1lb/4 cups unbleached strong
   white bread flour, plus a little extra
5ml/1 tsp salt
10g/¼oz fresh yeast or generous
   5ml/1 tsp active dried yeast
2.5ml/½ tsp light muscovado
   (brown) sugar
250ml/8fl oz/1 cup lukewarm water
60ml/4 tbsp extra virgin olive oil
5ml/1 tsp very finely chopped fresh
   rosemary, plus 6–8 small sprigs
1 red onion, halved and sliced
coarse sea salt

1 Sift the flour and salt into a bowl. Cream the fresh yeast with the sugar and slowly stir in half the water. If using dried yeast, stir the sugar into the water and then sprinkle the dried yeast over the surface. Set aside in a warm, not hot, place for 10 minutes, until frothy.

2 Add the yeast, the remaining water, 15ml/1 tbsp of the oil and the chopped rosemary to the flour. Mix to form a dough, then gather it into a ball and knead on a floured work surface for about 5 minutes, until smooth and elastic. You may need a little extra flour if the dough is very sticky.

3 Place the dough in a lightly oiled bowl, slip it into a plastic bag or cover with oiled clear film (plastic wrap) and leave to rise. Leave it all day in a cool place, overnight in the refrigerator, or for 1–2 hours in a warm place.

4 Lightly oil a baking sheet. Knead the dough to form a flat loaf about 30cm/12in round or square. Place on the baking sheet, cover with greased plastic or clear film and leave to rise in a warm place for 40–60 minutes.

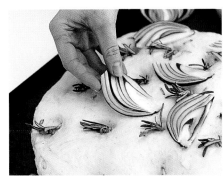

5 Preheat the oven to 220°C/425°F/Gas 7. Toss the onion in 15ml/1 tbsp of the oil and sprinkle over the loaf with the rosemary sprigs.

6 Drizzle the remaining oil over the loaf, then sprinkle with sea salt. Bake the focaccia for 15 minutes, then reduce the heat to 190°C/375°F/Gas 5 and cook for a further 10–15 minutes. Cool on a wire rack.

VARIATION

To make garlic and thyme focaccia, peel 1–2 heads of garlic but leave the cloves whole. Cook gently in 15–30ml/1–2 tbsp olive oil until lightly coloured, then cook in the oven at 180°C/350°F/Gas 4 for about 30 minutes, until soft, browned, but not at all burned. Stir once or twice during cooking, then leave to cool. When shaping the focaccia, gently knead in the caramelized garlic with about 5ml/1 tsp chopped fresh thyme. Omit the onion topping, but brush with more olive oil and sprinkle with fresh thyme sprigs and coarse sea salt. Bake as above.

ONION, PARMESAN AND OLIVE BREAD

THIS BREAD IS GOOD FOR SANDWICHES OR CUT INTO THICK SLICES AND DIPPED IN OLIVE OIL, THEN EATEN AS A SNACK. IT IS REALLY EXCELLENT WHEN TOASTED — FOR EXAMPLE, MAKING A WONDERFUL BASE FOR BRUSCHETTA OR DELICIOUS CROÛTONS FOR TOSSING INTO SALAD.

MAKES ONE LARGE/TWO SMALL LOAVES

INGREDIENTS

350g/12oz/3 cups strong white bread
   flour, plus a little extra
115g/4oz/1 cup yellow cornmeal,
   plus a little extra
rounded 5ml/1 tsp salt
15g/½oz fresh yeast or 10ml/2 tsp
   active dried yeast
5ml/1 tsp muscovado
   (molasses) sugar
270ml/9fl oz/generous 1 cup
   warm water
5ml/1 tsp chopped fresh thyme
30ml/2 tbsp olive oil
1 onion, finely chopped
75g/3oz/1 cup freshly grated
   Parmesan cheese
90g/3½oz/scant 1 cup pitted
   black olives, halved

1 Mix the flour, cornmeal and salt in a warmed bowl. If using fresh yeast, cream it with the sugar and gradually stir in 120ml/4fl oz/½ cup of the warm water. If using dried yeast, stir the sugar into the water and then sprinkle the dried yeast over the surface. Leave in a warm place for 10 minutes, until frothy.

2 Make a well in the centre of the dry ingredients and pour in the yeast liquid. Add the remaining warm water.

3 Add the chopped fresh thyme and 15ml/1 tbsp of the olive oil and mix thoroughly with a wooden spoon, gradually drawing in the dry ingredients until they are fully incorporated. Add a dash more warm water, if necessary, to make a soft, but not sticky, dough.

4 Knead the dough on a lightly floured work surface for 5 minutes, until smooth and elastic. Place in a clean, lightly oiled bowl and place in a plastic bag or cover with oiled clear film (plastic wrap). Set aside to rise in a warm place for 1–2 hours.

5 Meanwhile, heat the remaining olive oil in a heavy frying pan. Add the onion and cook over fairly gentle heat, stirring occasionally, for 8 minutes, until softened, but not at all browned. Set aside to cool.

6 Brush a baking sheet with olive oil. Turn out the dough on to a floured work surface. Gently knead in the onions, followed by the Parmesan and olives.

7 Shape the dough into one or two rough oval loaves. Sprinkle a little cornmeal on the work surface and roll the bread in it, then place on the prepared baking sheet. Make several slits across the top.

8 Slip the baking sheet into the plastic bag or cover with oiled clear film and leave to rise in a warm place for about 1 hour, or until well risen. Preheat the oven to 200°C/400°F/Gas 6. Bake for 30–35 minutes, or until the bread sounds hollow when tapped on the base. Cool on a wire rack.

VARIATION
Alternatively, shape the dough into a loaf, roll in cornmeal and place in an oiled loaf tin (pan). Leave to rise well above the rim of the tin, as in step 8. Bake for 35–40 minutes, or until the loaf sounds hollow when tapped.

We add onions to marinades, to stews and casseroles,

to roasts and braises, and we cook them in countless

ways to accompany simply grilled meat, poultry and fish.

Certain classics stand out: a steaming Seafood Laksa,

Coq au Vin and the hearty Gigot Boulangère.

Imagine liver with onions, burgers without relish or

stew without onion. In fact, it is hard to think of many

main meals in which onions aren't an essential ingredient.

Main Meals

CHINESE-STYLE STEAMED FISH

THIS IS A CLASSIC CHINESE WAY OF COOKING WHOLE FISH, WITH GARLIC, SPRING ONIONS, GINGER AND BLACK BEANS. THE FISH MAKES A SPLENDID CENTREPIECE FOR A CHINESE MEAL OR IT CAN BE SERVED MORE SIMPLY, WITH BOILED RICE AND SOME STIR-FRIED CHINESE GREENS.

SERVES FOUR TO SIX

INGREDIENTS

    2 sea bass, grey mullet or trout, each
      weighing about 675–800g/1½–1¾lb
    25ml/1½ tbsp salted black beans
    2.5ml/½ tsp sugar
    30ml/2 tbsp finely shredded fresh
      root ginger
    4 garlic cloves, thinly sliced
    30ml/2 tbsp Chinese rice wine or
      dry sherry
    30ml/2 tbsp light soy sauce
    4–6 spring onions (scallions), finely
      shredded or sliced diagonally
    45ml/3 tbsp groundnut (peanut) oil
    10ml/2 tsp sesame oil

1 Wash the fish inside and out under cold running water, then pat them dry on kitchen paper. Using a sharp knife, slash 3–4 deep cross shapes on each side of each fish.

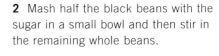

2 Mash half the black beans with the sugar in a small bowl and then stir in the remaining whole beans.

3 Place a little ginger and garlic inside the cavity of each fish and then lay them on a plate or dish that will fit inside a large steamer. Rub the bean mixture into the fish, especially into the slashes, then sprinkle the remaining ginger and garlic over the top. Cover and chill for 30 minutes.

4 Place the steamer over a pan of boiling water. Sprinkle the rice wine or sherry and half the soy sauce over the fish and steam them for 15–20 minutes, or until just cooked.

5 Drizzle with the remaining soy sauce and sprinkle the shredded or sliced spring onions over the fish.

6 In a small pan, heat the groundnut oil until smoking, then trickle it over the spring onions. Sprinkle with the sesame oil and serve immediately.

SEAFOOD LAKSA

A LAKSA IS A MALAYSIAN STEW OF FISH, POULTRY, MEAT OR VEGETABLES WITH NOODLES. AUTHENTIC LAKSAS ARE OFTEN VERY HOT, AND COOLED BY THE COCONUT MILK AND THE NOODLES. IF YOU WOULD PREFER A SPICY VERSION, ADD A LITTLE CHILLI POWDER INSTEAD OF SOME OF THE PAPRIKA.

SERVES FOUR TO FIVE

INGREDIENTS

3 medium-hot fresh red
  chillies, seeded
4–5 garlic cloves
5ml/1 tsp mild paprika
10ml/2 tsp fermented shrimp
  paste
25ml/1½ tbsp chopped fresh root
  ginger or galangal
250g/9oz small red shallots
25g/1oz fresh coriander (cilantro),
  preferably with roots
45ml/3 tbsp groundnut (peanut) oil
5ml/1 tsp fennel seeds, crushed
2 fennel bulbs, cut into thin wedges
600ml/1 pint/2½ cups fish stock
300g/11oz thin vermicelli
  rice noodles
450ml/¾ pint/scant 2 cups
  coconut milk
juice of 1–2 limes
30–45ml/2–3 tbsp Thai fish sauce
450g/1lb firm white fish fillet, such
  as monkfish, halibut or snapper
450g/1lb large raw prawns (shrimp),
  about 20, shelled and deveined
small bunch of fresh holy basil or
  ordinary basil
2 spring onions (scallions),
  thinly sliced

1 Process the chillies, garlic, paprika, shrimp paste, ginger or galangal and 2 shallots to a paste in a food processor, blender or spice grinder. Remove the roots and stems from the coriander and add them to the paste; chop and reserve the coriander leaves. Add 15ml/1 tbsp of the oil to the paste and process again until fairly smooth.

2 Heat the remaining oil in a large pan. Add the remaining shallots, the fennel seeds and fennel wedges. Cook until lightly browned, then add 45ml/3 tbsp of the paste and stir-fry for about 1–2 minutes. Pour in the fish stock and bring to the boil. Reduce the heat and simmer for 8–10 minutes.

3 Meanwhile, cook the vermicelli rice noodles according to the packet instructions. Drain and set aside.

4 Add the coconut milk and the juice of 1 lime to the pan of shallots. Stir in 30ml/2 tbsp of the fish sauce. Bring to a simmer and taste, adding a little more spice paste, lime juice or fish sauce as necessary.

5 Cut the fish into chunks and add to the pan. Cook for 2–3 minutes, then add the prawns and cook until they turn pink. Chop most of the basil and add to the pan with the reserved coriander.

6 Divide the noodles among 4–5 wide bowls, then ladle in the stew. Sprinkle with spring onions and the remaining whole basil leaves. Serve immediately.

GRILLED SOLE <u>WITH</u> CHIVE <u>AND</u> LEMON GRASS BUTTER

CHIVES ARE AT THEIR BEST WHEN BARELY COOKED, AND THEY MAKE A DELICIOUS BUTTER TO SERVE WITH SIMPLE GRILLED FISH. SOLE IS THE IDEAL CHOICE, BUT HALIBUT, TURBOT AND SWORDFISH ARE ALSO GOOD. SERVE WITH STEAMED NEW POTATOES AND A SIMPLE VEGETABLE ACCOMPANIMENT.

SERVES FOUR

INGREDIENTS
115g/4oz/½ cup unsalted (sweet) butter, plus extra melted butter
5ml/1 tsp minced (ground) lemon grass
pinch of finely grated lime rind
1 kaffir lime leaf, very finely shredded (optional)
45ml/3 tbsp chopped chives or chopped chive flowers, plus extra chives or chive flowers to garnish
2.5–5ml/½–1 tsp Thai fish sauce
4 sole, skinned
salt and ground black pepper
lemon or lime wedges, to serve

COOK'S TIP
Thai fish sauce, also known as *nam pla*, is available from Asian food stores.

1 Cream the butter with the lemon grass, lime rind, lime leaf, if using, and chives or chive flowers. Season to taste with Thai fish sauce, salt and pepper.

2 Chill the butter mixture to firm it, then form it into a roll and wrap in foil or clear film (plastic wrap). Chill until firm. Preheat the grill (broiler).

3 Brush the fish with a little melted butter. Place it on the grill rack and season. Grill (broil) for about 5 minutes on each side, until firm and just cooked. Meanwhile, cut the chilled butter into thin slices. Serve the fish immediately, topped with slices of the butter. Garnish with chives. Offer lemon or lime wedges with the fish.

SEARED TUNA STEAKS
WITH RED ONION SALSA

RED ONIONS ARE IDEAL FOR THIS SALSA, NOT ONLY FOR THEIR MILD AND SWEET FLAVOUR, BUT ALSO BECAUSE THEY LOOK SO APPETIZING. SALAD, RICE OR BREAD AND A BOWL OF THICK YOGURT FLAVOURED WITH CHOPPED FRESH HERBS ARE GOOD ACCOMPANIMENTS.

SERVES FOUR

INGREDIENTS

4 tuna loin steaks, each weighing
  about 175–200g/6–7oz
5ml/1 tsp cumin seeds, toasted
  and crushed
pinch of dried red chilli flakes
grated rind and juice of 1 lime
30–60ml/2–4 tbsp extra virgin
  olive oil
salt and ground black pepper
lime wedges and fresh coriander
  (cilantro) sprigs, to garnish

For the salsa

1 small red onion, finely chopped
200g/7oz red or yellow cherry
  tomatoes, coarsely chopped
1 avocado, peeled, stoned (pitted)
  and chopped
2 kiwi fruit, peeled and chopped
1 fresh red chilli, seeded and
  finely chopped
15g/½oz/½ cup fresh coriander
  (cilantro), chopped
6 fresh mint sprigs, leaves
  only, chopped
5–10ml/1–2 tsp Thai fish sauce
about 5ml/1 tsp muscovado
  (molasses) sugar

1 Wash the tuna steaks and pat dry. Sprinkle with half the cumin, the dried chilli, salt, pepper and half the lime rind. Rub in 30ml/2 tbsp of the oil and set aside in a glass or china dish for about 30 minutes.

2 Meanwhile, make the salsa. Mix the onion, tomatoes, avocado, kiwi fruit, fresh chilli, chopped coriander and mint. Add the remaining cumin, the rest of the lime rind and half the lime juice. Add Thai fish sauce and sugar to taste. Set aside for 15–20 minutes, then add more Thai fish sauce, lime juice and olive oil if required.

3 Heat a ridged, cast iron griddle pan. Cook the tuna, allowing about 2 minutes on each side for rare tuna or a little longer for a medium result.

4 Serve the tuna steaks garnished with lime wedges and coriander sprigs. Serve the salsa separately or spoon on to the plates with the tuna.

BACON-WRAPPED TROUT <u>WITH</u> OATMEAL <u>AND</u> ONION STUFFING

THIS STUFFING IS BASED ON A SCOTTISH SPECIALITY, A MIXTURE OF OATMEAL AND ONION CALLED SKIRLIE. HERRING CAN BE COOKED IN THE SAME WAY. THIS IS VERY GOOD WITH SLICES OF COOKED POTATOES, BRUSHED WITH OLIVE OIL AND GRILLED UNTIL GOLDEN ON EACH SIDE.

SERVES FOUR

INGREDIENTS
  10 dry-cured streaky (fatty) bacon
    rashers (strips)
  40g/1½oz/3 tbsp butter or bacon fat
  1 onion, finely chopped
  115g/4oz/1 cup oatmeal
  30ml/2 tbsp chopped fresh parsley
  30ml/2 tbsp chopped fresh chives
  4 trout, about 350g/12oz each,
    gutted and boned
  juice of ½ lemon
  salt and ground black pepper
  watercress, cherry tomatoes and
    lemon wedges, to serve
For the herb mayonnaise
  6 watercress sprigs
  15ml/1 tbsp chopped fresh chives
  30ml/2 tbsp coarsely chopped
    fresh parsley
  90ml/6 tbsp lemon mayonnaise
  30ml/2 tbsp crème fraîche
  2.5–5ml/½–1 tsp tarragon mustard

3 Wash and dry the trout, then stuff with the oatmeal mixture. Wrap each fish in 2 bacon rashers and place in an ovenproof dish. Dot with the remaining butter and sprinkle with the lemon juice. Bake for 20–25 minutes, until the bacon browns and crisps a little.

4 Meanwhile, make the mayonnaise. Place the watercress, chives and parsley in a sieve and pour boiling water over them. Drain, rinse under cold water, and drain well on kitchen paper.

5 Purée the herbs in a mortar with a pestle. (This is easier than using a food processor for this small quantity.) Stir the puréed herbs into the lemon mayonnaise together with the crème fraîche. Add tarragon mustard to taste and stir to combine.

6 When cooked, transfer the trout to warmed serving plates and serve immediately with watercress, tomatoes and lemon wedges, accompanied by the herb mayonnaise.

1 Preheat the oven to 190°C/375°F/ Gas 5. Chop 2 of the bacon rashers. Melt 25g/1oz/2 tbsp of the butter or bacon fat in a large frying pan and cook the bacon briefly. Add the finely chopped onion and cook gently for 5–8 minutes, until softened.

2 Add the oatmeal and cook until the oatmeal darkens and absorbs the fat, but do not allow it to overbrown. Stir in the parsley, chives and seasoning. Cool.

BAKED MONKFISH WITH POTATOES AND GARLIC

THIS SIMPLE SUPPER DISH CAN BE MADE WITH OTHER FISH. SAUCE TARTARE OR A THICK VINAIGRETTE FLAVOURED WITH CHOPPED GHERKINS AND HARD-BOILED EGG ARE DELICIOUS ACCOMPANIMENTS.

SERVES FOUR

INGREDIENTS
   1kg/2¼lb waxy potatoes, cut
     into chunks
   50g/2oz/¼ cup butter
   2 onions, thickly sliced
   4 garlic cloves
   few fresh thyme sprigs
   2–3 fresh bay leaves
   450ml/¾ pint/scant 2 cups
     vegetable or fish stock,
     plus 45ml/3 tbsp
   900g/2lb monkfish tail in one piece,
     skin and membrane removed
   30–45ml/2–3 tbsp white wine
   50g/2oz/1 cup fresh
     white breadcrumbs
   15g/½oz/½ cup fresh
     parsley, chopped
   15ml/1 tbsp olive oil
   salt and ground black pepper

1 Preheat the oven to 190°C/375°F/ Gas 5. Put the potatoes in an ovenproof dish. Melt half the butter in a large frying pan and cook the onions gently for 5–6 minutes. Add to the dish.

2 Slice 2–3 of the garlic cloves and add to the potatoes with the thyme and bay leaves, and season with salt and freshly ground black pepper.

3 Pour in the main batch of stock over the potatoes and bake, stirring once or twice, for 50–60 minutes, until the potatoes are just tender.

4 Nestle the monkfish into the potatoes and season with salt and pepper. Bake for 10–15 minutes. Mix the 45ml/3 tbsp stock with the wine and use to baste the monkfish 2–3 times during cooking.

5 Finely chop the remaining garlic. Melt the remaining butter and toss it with the breadcrumbs, chopped garlic, most of the chopped parsley and seasoning. Spoon over the monkfish, pressing it down gently with the back of a spoon.

6 Drizzle the olive oil over the crumb-covered fish, return the dish to the oven and bake for a final 10–15 minutes, until the breadcrumbs are crisp and golden and all the liquid has been absorbed. Sprinkle the remaining parsley on to the potatoes and serve immediately.

PISSALADIÈRE

THIS FAMOUS ONION AND ANCHOVY DISH IS A TRADITIONAL MARKET FOOD OF NICE IN SOUTHERN FRANCE. IT CAN BE MADE USING EITHER SHORTCRUST PASTRY OR, AS HERE, YEASTED DOUGH, SIMILAR TO A PIZZA BASE. EITHER WAY, IT IS MOST DELICIOUS EATEN LUKEWARM RATHER THAN PIPING HOT.

SERVES SIX

INGREDIENTS
   250g/9oz/2¼ cups strong white bread
      flour, plus extra for dusting
   50g/2oz/⅓ cup fine polenta
      or semolina
   5ml/1 tsp salt
   175ml/6fl oz/¾ cup lukewarm water
   5ml/1 tsp dried yeast
   5ml/1 tsp caster (superfine) sugar
   30ml/2 tbsp extra virgin olive oil
For the topping
   60–75ml/4–5 tbsp extra virgin
      olive oil
   6 large sweet Spanish (Bermuda)
      onions, thinly sliced
   2 large garlic cloves, thinly sliced
   5ml/1 tsp chopped fresh thyme, plus
      several sprigs
   1 fresh rosemary sprig
   1–2 × 50g/2oz cans anchovies in
      olive oil
   50–75g/2–3oz small black olives,
      preferably small Niçoise olives
   salt and ground black pepper

1 Mix the flour, polenta or semolina and salt in a large mixing bowl. Pour half the water into a bowl. Add the yeast and sugar, then leave in a warm place for 10 minutes, until frothy. Pour the yeast mixture into the flour mixture with the remaining water and the olive oil.

2 Using your hands, mix all the ingredients together to form a dough, then turn out and knead for 5 minutes, until smooth, springy and elastic.

3 Return the dough to the clean, floured bowl and place it in a plastic bag or cover with oiled clear film (plastic wrap), then set the dough aside at room temperature for 30–60 minutes to rise and double in bulk.

4 Meanwhile, start to prepare the topping. Heat 45ml/3 tbsp of the olive oil in a large, heavy pan and add the sliced onions. Stir well to coat the onions in the oil, then cover the pan and cook over a very low heat, stirring occasionally, for 20-30 minutes. (Use a heat-diffuser mat to keep the heat low, if possible.)

5 Add a little salt to taste and the garlic, chopped thyme and rosemary sprig. Stir well and continue cooking for another 15–25 minutes, or until the onions are soft and deep golden yellow but not browned at all. Uncover the pan for the last 5–10 minutes' cooking if the onions seem very wet. Remove and discard the rosemary. Set the onions aside to cool.

6 Preheat the oven to 220°C/425°F/ Gas 7. Roll out the dough thinly and use to line a large baking sheet, about 30 × 23–25cm/12 × 9–10in. Taste the onions for seasoning before spreading them over the dough.

7 Drain the anchovies, cut them in half lengthways and arrange them in a lattice pattern over the onions. Sprinkle the olives and thyme sprigs over the top of the pissaladière and drizzle with the remaining olive oil. Bake for about 20–25 minutes, or until the dough is browned and cooked. Season with pepper and serve warm, cut into slices.

VARIATIONS
• Shortcrust pastry can be used instead of yeast dough as a base: bake it blind for 10–15 minutes before adding the filling.
• If you enjoy anchovies, try spreading about 60ml/4 tbsp anchovy purée (paste) – *anchoïade* – over the base before adding the onions. Alternatively, spread black olive paste over the base.

GUINEA FOWL <u>AND</u> SPRING VEGETABLE STEW

MILD, SWEET LEEKS ARE EXCELLENT IN THIS LIGHT STEW OF GUINEA FOWL AND SPRING VEGETABLES.
CHICKEN OR RABBIT PIECES CAN BE USED INSTEAD OF GUINEA FOWL.

SERVES FOUR

INGREDIENTS
45ml/3 tbsp olive oil
115g/4oz pancetta, cut into lardons
30ml/2 tbsp plain (all-purpose) flour
2 × 1.2–1.6kg/2½–3½lb guinea fowl,
  each cut in 4 portions
1 onion, chopped
cloves from 1 head of garlic, peeled
1 bottle dry white wine
fresh thyme sprig
1 fresh bay leaf
a few parsley stalks
250g/9oz baby carrots
250g/9oz baby turnips
6 slender leeks, cut into 7.5cm/
  3in lengths
250g/9oz shelled peas
15ml/1 tbsp French herb mustard
15g/½oz/½ cup fresh flat leaf
  parsley, chopped
15ml/1 tbsp chopped fresh mint
salt and ground black pepper

1 Heat 30ml/2 tbsp of the oil in a large frying pan and cook the pancetta over a medium heat until lightly browned, stirring occasionally. Remove the pancetta from the pan and set aside.

2 Season the flour with salt and pepper and toss the guinea fowl portions in it. Cook in the oil remaining in the pan until browned on all sides. Transfer to a flameproof casserole. Preheat the oven to 180°C/350°F/Gas 4.

3 Add the remaining oil to the pan and cook the onion gently until soft. Add the garlic and cook for 3–4 minutes, then stir in the pancetta and the wine.

4 Tie the thyme, bay leaf and parsley into a bundle and add to the pan. Bring to the boil, then simmer gently for 3–4 minutes. Pour over the guinea fowl and add seasoning. Cover and cook in the oven for 40 minutes.

5 Add the baby carrots and turnips to the casserole and cook, covered, for a further 30 minutes, or until the vegetables are just tender.

6 Stir in the leeks and cook for a further 15–20 minutes, or until all the vegetables are fully cooked.

7 Meanwhile, blanch the peas in boiling water for 2 minutes, then drain. Transfer the guinea fowl and vegetables to a warmed serving dish. Place the casserole on the hob (stovetop) and boil the juices vigorously over a high heat until they are reduced by about half.

8 Stir in the peas and cook gently for 2–3 minutes, then stir in the mustard and adjust the seasoning. Stir in most of the parsley and the mint. Pour this sauce over the guinea fowl or return it and the vegetables to the casserole. Sprinkle the remaining parsley over the top and serve immediately.

CHICKEN FAJITAS WITH GRILLED ONIONS

GRILLED MARINATED CHICKEN AND ONIONS, SERVED WITH SOFT TORTILLAS, SALSA, GUACAMOLE AND SOUR CREAM, MAKES A CLASSIC TEX-MEX MEAL AND IS A GOOD CHOICE FOR AN INFORMAL SUPPER.

SERVES SIX

INGREDIENTS

    finely grated rind of 1 lime and the
      juice of 2 limes
    120ml/4fl oz/½ cup olive oil
    1 garlic clove, finely chopped
    2.5ml/½ tsp dried oregano
    good pinch of dried red chilli flakes
    5ml/1 tsp coriander seeds, crushed
    6 boneless chicken breast portions
    3 Spanish (Bermuda) onions, sliced
    2 large red, yellow or orange (bell)
      peppers, seeded and cut into strips
    30ml/2 tbsp chopped fresh
      coriander (cilantro)
    salt and ground black pepper
For the salsa
    450g/1lb tomatoes, peeled, seeded
      and chopped
    2 garlic cloves, finely chopped
    1 small red onion, finely chopped
    1–2 green chillies, seeded and
      finely chopped
    finely grated rind of ½ lime
    30ml/2 tbsp chopped fresh coriander
    pinch of caster (superfine) sugar
    2.5–5ml/½–1 tsp ground toasted
      cumin seeds
To serve
    12–18 soft flour tortillas
    guacamole
    120ml/4fl oz/½ cup sour cream
    crisp lettuce leaves
    fresh coriander sprigs
    lime wedges

1 In an ovenproof dish, combine the lime rind and juice, 75ml/5 tbsp of the oil, the garlic, oregano, chilli flakes and coriander seeds, and season with salt and pepper. Slash the skin on the chicken portions several times and turn them in the mixture, then cover and set aside to marinate for several hours.

2 To make the salsa, combine the tomatoes, garlic, onion, chillies, lime rind and crushed coriander. Season to taste with salt, pepper, sugar and cumin. Set aside for 30 minutes, then taste and adjust the seasoning.

3 Heat the grill (broiler). Thread the onion slices on to a skewer or place on a grill rack. Brush with 15ml/1 tbsp of the oil and season. Grill (broil) until softened and charred in places. Preheat the oven to 200°C/400°F/Gas 6.

4 Cook the chicken portions in their marinade, covered, in the oven for 20 minutes. Remove from the oven, then grill the chicken for 8–10 minutes, until browned and fully cooked.

5 Meanwhile, heat the remaining oil in a large frying pan and cook the peppers for about 10 minutes, until softened and browned in places. Add the grilled onions and cook for 2–3 minutes.

6 Add the chicken cooking juices and cook over a high heat, stirring frequently, until the liquid evaporates. Stir in the chopped coriander.

7 Warm the tortillas following the instructions on the packet. Using a sharp knife, cut the grilled chicken into strips and transfer to a serving dish. Place the onion and pepper mixture and the salsa in separate dishes.

8 Serve the dishes of chicken, onions and peppers and salsa with the tortillas, guacamole, sour cream, lettuce and coriander for people to help themselves. Serve lime wedges so that the juice can be squeezed over to taste.

COQ ^{AU} VIN

THIS IS A FAMOUS BURGUNDIAN RECIPE THAT IS GARNISHED WITH LITTLE ONIONS AND MUSHROOMS.
IT WAS THE HEIGHT OF FASHION IN THE 1960S AND IT IS BACK IN VOGUE AGAIN.

SERVES FOUR

INGREDIENTS

1 celery stick
1 fresh bay leaf
fresh thyme sprig
1 bottle full-bodied red wine (Shiraz
  or Zinfandel would be good)
600ml/1 pint/2½ cups good
  chicken stock
50g/2oz/¼ cup butter
30ml/2 tbsp olive oil
24 small pickling onions
115g/4oz piece of bacon or
  unsmoked pancetta, cut
  into lardons
45ml/3 tbsp plain (all-purpose) flour
2.25kg/5lb chicken, cut
  into 8 pieces
45ml/3 tbsp Cognac
2 garlic cloves, chopped
15ml/1 tbsp tomato purée (paste)
piece of fresh pork skin, about
  15cm/6in square (optional)
250g/9oz button (white) mushrooms
30ml/2 tbsp chopped fresh parsley
salt and ground black pepper
croûtons, to garnish (optional)

1 Tie the celery, bay leaf and thyme together in a bundle and place in a pan. Pour in the wine and stock and simmer, uncovered, for 15 minutes.

2 Melt 15g/½oz/1 tbsp of the butter with half the olive oil in a heavy frying pan and brown 16 of the onions all over. Use a slotted spoon to transfer the onions to a plate.

3 Add the bacon or pancetta and cook until browned, then set aside.

COOK'S TIP
For a really good flavour, complete the casserole up to the end of step 8, then cool and leave in the refrigerator overnight. Next day, skim off the excess fat from the top of the casserole and reheat gently on the hob for 20 minutes before finishing steps 9–11.

4 Meanwhile, season 30ml/2 tbsp of the flour with salt and pepper. Dust the chicken pieces with the seasoned flour and cook them in the fat remaining in the pan over a medium heat, turning frequently, for about 10 minutes, or until golden brown all over.

5 Pour in the Cognac and carefully set it alight using a long match or taper. When the flames have died down, remove the chicken from the pan and set aside.

6 Chop the remaining onions. Add another 15g/½oz/1 tbsp of the butter to the frying pan and cook the chopped onions with the garlic over a medium heat, stirring frequently, for 5 minutes, until softened and just turning brown. Preheat the oven to 190°C/375°F/Gas 5.

7 Add the wine and stock mixture, with the herb bundle, and stir in the tomato purée. Lower the heat, then simmer gently, stirring frequently, for about 20 minutes. Taste and adjust the seasoning, if necessary.

8 Place the pork skin, if using, rind side down in a flameproof casserole, then add the chicken pieces and bacon or pancetta. Pour in the sauce (with the bundle of herbs). Cover and place in the oven. Reduce the temperature to 160°C/325°F/Gas 3 immediately and cook for 1½ hours. Add the whole browned onions and cook for a further 30 minutes.

9 Meanwhile, cook the mushrooms in another 15g/½oz/1 tbsp butter and the remaining oil until browned. Set them aside. Mix the remaining butter and flour to make a paste (known in French as *beurre manié*).

10 Using a slotted spoon, transfer the chicken and onions to a serving plate. Discard the pork skin from the casserole and heat the cooking juices on the hob (stovetop) until simmering. Add the *beurre manié* in small lumps, whisking to blend the paste into the sauce as it melts. Continue adding small pieces of paste, allowing each to melt completely before adding the next, until the simmering sauce is thickened to taste. (You may not need to use all the *beurre manié*.)

11 Add the mushrooms and cook for a few minutes. Pour the sauce over the chicken and sprinkle with chopped parsley. Garnish with croûtons, if using, and serve immediately.

BRAISED PORK CHOPS WITH ONION AND MUSTARD SAUCE

THE PIQUANT SAUCE ADDS PUNCH AND EXTRA FLAVOUR TO THIS SIMPLE SUPPER DISH. SERVE IT WITH CELERIAC AND POTATO MASH AND A GREEN VEGETABLE, SUCH AS BROCCOLI OR CABBAGE.

SERVES FOUR

INGREDIENTS
   4 pork loin chops, at least
      2cm/¾in thick
   30ml/2 tbsp plain (all-purpose) flour
   45ml/3 tbsp olive oil
   2 Spanish (Bermuda) onions, sliced
   2 garlic cloves, finely chopped
   250ml/8fl oz/1 cup dry (hard) cider
   150ml/¼ pint/⅔ cup vegetable,
      chicken or pork stock
   generous pinch of brown sugar
   2 fresh bay leaves
   6 fresh thyme sprigs
   2 strips lemon rind
   120ml/4fl oz/½ cup double
      (heavy) cream
   30–45ml/2–3 tbsp Meaux mustard
   30ml/2 tbsp chopped fresh parsley
   salt and ground black pepper

1 Preheat the oven to 200°C/400°F/ Gas 6. Trim the chops of excess fat. Season the flour with salt and pepper and use to coat the chops. Heat 30ml/ 2 tbsp of the oil in a frying pan and brown the chops on both sides, then transfer them to an ovenproof dish.

2 Add the remaining oil to the pan and cook the onions over a fairly gentle heat until they soften and begin to brown at the edges. Add the garlic and cook for 2 minutes more.

3 Stir in any left-over flour, then gradually stir in the cider and stock. Season well with salt and pepper and add the brown sugar, bay leaves, thyme sprigs and lemon rind. Bring the sauce to the boil, stirring constantly, then pour over the chops.

4 Cover and cook in the oven for 20 minutes. Reduce the heat to 180°C/ 350°F/Gas 4 and continue cooking for another 30–40 minutes. Remove the foil for the last 10 minutes of the cooking time. Remove the chops from the dish and keep warm, covered with foil.

5 Tip the remaining contents of the dish into a pan or, if the dish is flameproof, place it over a direct heat. Discard the herbs and lemon rind, then bring to the boil.

6 Add the cream and continue to boil, stirring constantly. Taste for seasoning, adding a pinch more sugar if necessary. Finally, stir in the mustard to taste and pour the sauce over the braised chops. Sprinkle with the chopped parsley and serve immediately.

VARIATION
For a less rich sauce, omit the cream and process the sauce in a blender. Reheat, thinning with a little extra stock if necessary, then adjust the seasoning and add mustard to taste. This will produce a sharper tasting sauce that will need less mustard.

BOILED BACON WITH ONION AND CAPER SAUCE

ONIONS AND CAPERS MAKE A PIQUANT SAUCE THAT IS TRADITIONAL WITH BOILED MUTTON, BUT IT IS ALSO DELICIOUS WITH BOILED BACON OR GAMMON. SERVE WITH SMALL NEW POTATOES, SAUTÉED WITH BUTTER AND A LITTLE GARLIC, AND BROAD BEANS TO MAKE A SPLENDID MEAL.

SERVES SIX

INGREDIENTS
- 1.8–2kg/4–4½lb gammon (smoked or cured ham) or bacon joint (roast)
- 4 cloves
- 1 onion, quartered
- 1 large carrot, sliced
- 1 celery stick
- 1 fresh bay leaf
- fresh thyme sprig
- 30ml/2 tbsp Dijon mustard
- 45–60ml/3–4 tbsp demerara (raw brown) sugar

For the sauce
- 50g/2oz/¼ cup butter
- 225g/8oz onions, chopped
- 60ml/4 tbsp plain (all-purpose) flour
- 250ml/8fl oz/1 cup milk
- 1 fresh bay leaf
- 30ml/2 tbsp small salted capers, rinsed and coarsely chopped
- 30ml/2 tbsp chopped fresh parsley
- 15–30ml/1–2 tbsp Dijon mustard
- salt and ground black pepper

1 Place the meat in a large pan and cover with cold water. Bring to the boil and simmer for 5 minutes. Drain, rinse, then return the meat to the pan and cover with fresh water. Stick the cloves into the onion and add to the pan with the carrot. Tie the celery, bay leaf and thyme together and add to the pan. Bring to the boil, then part-cover and simmer very gently for 25 minutes per 450g/1lb.

2 Preheat the oven to 200°C/400°F/Gas 6. Drain the gammon or bacon, reserving 475ml/16fl oz/2 cups of the cooking liquid. Place the meat in a roasting pan and strip off and discard the skin. Spread the mustard over the fat and press the sugar all over it.

3 Cook in the oven for 20–25 minutes, until glazed and browned. Keep warm, covered in foil, until ready to serve.

4 Start making the sauce just before the meat has finished boiling. Melt 40g/1½oz/3 tbsp of the butter in a heavy pan and cook the onions very gently, half-covered, for 20 minutes, until soft and yellow but not browned. Stir occasionally.

5 Stir in the flour and cook, stirring constantly, for 2–3 minutes. Gradually stir in 300ml/½ pint/1¼ cups of the hot reserved cooking liquid. Cook until the sauce is thick and smooth, then gradually stir in the milk. Add the bay leaf and cook very gently for 20–25 minutes, stirring frequently.

6 Gradually stir in a little more of the reserved cooking liquid to make a sauce of pouring consistency,∆ and cook for a further 5 minutes. Remove the bay leaf. Stir in the chopped capers and parsley. Add 15ml/1 tbsp mustard, then taste for seasoning. Add salt, pepper and more mustard to taste. Stir in the remaining butter and serve immediately with the sliced meat.

PORK CASSEROLE <u>WITH</u> ONIONS, CHILLI <u>AND</u> DRIED FRUIT

INSPIRED BY SOUTH AMERICAN COOKING, A MOLE – PASTE – OF CHILLI, SHALLOTS AND NUTS IS ADDED TO THIS CASSEROLE OF PORK AND ONIONS. PART OF THE MOLE IS ADDED AT THE END OF COOKING TO RETAIN ITS FRESH FLAVOUR. SERVE WITH RICE AND A GREEN SALAD.

SERVES SIX

INGREDIENTS
  25ml/5 tsp plain (all-purpose) flour
  1kg/2¼lb shoulder or leg of pork,
    cut into 5cm/2in cubes
  45–60ml/3–4 tbsp olive oil
  2 large onions, chopped
  2 garlic cloves, finely chopped
  600ml/1 pint/2½ cups fruity
    white wine
  105ml/7 tbsp water
  115g/4oz ready-to-eat prunes
  115g/4oz ready-to-eat
    dried apricots
  grated rind and juice of
    1 small orange
  pinch of muscovado (molasses) sugar
  30ml/2 tbsp chopped fresh parsley
  ½–1 fresh green chilli, seeded and
    finely chopped (optional)
  salt and ground black pepper
For the mole
  3 *ancho* chillies and 2 *pasilla* chillies
    (or other varieties of large, medium-
    hot dried red chillies)
  30ml/2 tbsp olive oil
  2 shallots, chopped
  2 garlic cloves, chopped
  1 fresh green chilli, seeded
    and chopped
  10ml/2 tsp ground coriander
  5ml/1 tsp mild Spanish paprika
    or *pimentón*
  50g/2oz/½ cup blanched
    almonds, toasted
  15ml/1 tbsp chopped fresh oregano
    or 2.5ml/½ tsp dried oregano

1 Make the mole paste first. Toast the dried chillies in a dry frying pan over a low heat for 1–2 minutes, until they are aromatic, then soak them in warm water for 30 minutes.

2 Drain the chillies, reserving the soaking water, and discard their stalks and seeds. Preheat the oven to 160°C/325°F/Gas 3.

3 Heat the oil in a small frying pan and cook the shallots, garlic, fresh green chilli and ground coriander over a very low heat for 5 minutes.

4 Transfer the shallot mixture to a food processor or blender and add the drained chillies, paprika or *pimentón*, almonds and oregano. Process the mixture, adding 45–60ml/3–4 tbsp of the chilli soaking liquid to make a workable paste.

5 Season the flour with salt and black pepper, then use to coat the pork. Heat 45ml/3 tbsp of the olive oil in a large, heavy frying pan and cook the pork, stirring frequently, until sealed on all sides. Transfer the pork cubes to a flameproof casserole.

6 If necessary, add the remaining oil to the frying pan and cook the onions and garlic gently for 8–10 minutes, stirring occasionally.

7 Add the wine and water to the frying pan. Cook for 2 minutes. Stir in half the mole paste, bring back to the boil and bubble for a few seconds before pouring over the pork.

8 Season lightly with salt and pepper and stir to mix, then cover and cook in the oven for 1½ hours.

9 Increase the oven temperature to 180°C/350°F/Gas 4. Stir in the prunes, apricots and orange juice. Taste and adjust the seasoning, add the muscovado sugar, cover and cook for another 30–45 minutes.

10 Place the casserole over a direct heat and stir in the remaining mole paste. Simmer, stirring once or twice, for 5 minutes. Serve sprinkled with the orange rind, chopped parsley and fresh chilli, if using.

GIGOT BOULANGÈRE

LAMB COOKED IN THE STYLE OF THE BAKER'S WIFE (LA BOULANGÈRE) IS A CLASSIC OF FRENCH PROVINCIAL COOKING. ONE OF THE BEST-KNOWN AND BEST-LOVED PAIRINGS OF LAMB AND GARLIC, THIS IS A TROUBLE-FREE AND DELICIOUS CHOICE FOR SUNDAY LUNCH.

4 Pour in the hot stock and add a little hot water, if necessary, to bring the liquid to just below the level of the potatoes. Dot with the remaining butter, cover them with foil and cook in the oven for 40 minutes. Increase the oven temperature to 200°C/400°F/Gas 6.

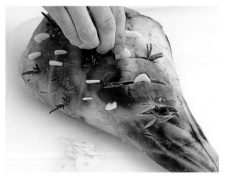

5 Meanwhile, cut the rest of the garlic into slivers. Make slits all over the lamb with a narrow, sharp knife and insert slivers of garlic and sprigs of thyme or rosemary into the slits. Season the lamb well with salt and pepper.

6 Uncover the potatoes and sprinkle a few rosemary or thyme sprigs over them. Rest a roasting rack or ovenproof cooling rack over the dish and place the lamb on it. Rub the olive oil over the meat, then return the dish to the oven. Cook, turning the lamb once or twice, for 1½–1¾ hours, depending on how well done you prefer lamb. Leave the lamb to rest for 20 minutes in a warm place (in the switched-off oven, for example) before carving.

SERVES SIX

INGREDIENTS
  50g/2oz/¼ cup butter, plus extra
    for greasing
  4–6 garlic cloves
  2 yellow onions, thinly sliced
  12–18 small fresh thyme or
    rosemary sprigs
  2 fresh bay leaves
  1.8kg/4lb red potatoes, thinly sliced
  450ml/¾ pint/scant 2 cups hot lamb
    or vegetable stock
  2kg/4½lb leg of lamb
  30ml/2 tbsp olive oil
  salt and ground black pepper

1 Preheat the oven to 190°C/375°F/Gas 5. Use a little butter to grease a large ovenproof dish, about 6cm/2½in deep. Finely chop half the garlic and sprinkle a little over the prepared dish.

2 Cook the onions in 25g/1oz/2 tbsp of the butter for 5–8 minutes, until softened. Coarsely chop half the thyme or rosemary and crush the bay leaves.

3 Arrange a layer of potatoes in the dish, season and sprinkle with half the remaining chopped garlic, rosemary or thyme, 1 bay leaf and the onions. Add the remaining potatoes, chopped garlic and herbs.

LAMB BURGERS WITH RED ONION AND TOMATO RELISH

A SHARP-SWEET RED ONION RELISH WORKS WELL WITH BURGERS BASED ON MIDDLE-EASTERN STYLE LAMB. SERVE WITH PITTA BREAD AND TABBOULEH OR WITH CHIPS AND A CRISP GREEN SALAD.

SERVES FOUR

INGREDIENTS

25g/1oz/3 tbsp bulgur wheat
500g/1¼lb lean minced
    (ground) lamb
1 small red onion, finely chopped
2 garlic cloves, finely chopped
1 green chilli, seeded and
    finely chopped
5ml/1 tsp ground toasted cumin seeds
2.5ml/½ tsp ground sumac
15g/½oz/½ cup fresh flat leaf
    parsley, chopped
30ml/2 tbsp chopped fresh mint
olive oil, for frying
salt and ground black pepper

For the relish

2 red (bell) peppers, halved
    and seeded
2 red onions, cut into 5mm/¼in
    thick slices
75–90ml/5–6 tbsp extra virgin olive oil
350g/12oz cherry tomatoes, chopped
½–1 fresh red or green chilli, seeded
    and finely chopped (optional)
30ml/2 tbsp chopped fresh mint
30ml/2 tbsp chopped fresh parsley
15ml/1 tbsp chopped fresh oregano
2.5–5ml/½–1 tsp each ground toasted
    cumin seeds
2.5–5ml/½–1 tsp sumac
juice of ½ lemon
caster (superfine) sugar, to taste

1 Pour 150ml/¼ pint/⅔ cup hot water over the bulgur wheat in a bowl and leave to stand for 15 minutes, then drain in a sieve and squeeze out the excess moisture.

2 Place the bulgur wheat in a bowl and add the minced lamb, onion, garlic, chilli, cumin, sumac, parsley and mint. Mix the ingredients thoroughly together by hand, then season with 5ml/1 tsp salt and plenty of black pepper and mix again. Form the mixture into 8 small burgers and set aside while you make the relish.

3 Grill (broil) the peppers, skin side up, until the skin chars and blisters. Place in a bowl, cover and leave to stand for 10 minutes. Peel off the skin, dice the peppers finely and place in a bowl.

4 Brush the onions with 15ml/1 tbsp oil and grill for 5 minutes on each side, until browned. Cool, then chop.

5 Add the onions, tomatoes, chilli to taste, the mint, parsley, oregano and 2.5ml/½ tsp each of the cumin and sumac to the peppers. Stir in 60ml/4 tbsp of the remaining oil and 15ml/1 tbsp of the lemon juice. Season with salt, pepper and sugar and leave to stand for 20–30 minutes.

6 Heat a heavy frying pan or a ridged griddle pan over a high heat and grease lightly with olive oil. Cook the burgers for about 5–6 minutes on each side, or until just cooked at the centre.

7 While the burgers are cooking, taste the relish and adjust the seasoning, adding more salt, pepper, sugar, oil, chilli, cumin, sumac and lemon juice to taste. Serve the burgers immediately as they are cooked, with the relish.

LAMB STEW <u>WITH</u> BABY ONIONS <u>AND</u> NEW POTATOES

THIS FRESH LEMON-SEASONED STEW IS FINISHED WITH AN ITALIAN MIXTURE OF CHOPPED GARLIC, PARSLEY AND LEMON RIND KNOWN AS GREMOLATA, THE TRADITIONAL TOPPING FOR OSSO BUCCO.

SERVES SIX

INGREDIENTS
    1kg/2¼lb boneless shoulder of lamb,
      trimmed of fat and cut into 5cm/
      2in cubes
    1 garlic clove, finely chopped
    finely grated rind of ½ lemon and
      juice of 1 lemon
    90ml/6 tbsp olive oil
    45ml/3 tbsp plain (all-purpose) flour
    1 large onion, sliced
    5 anchovy fillets in olive oil, drained
    2.5ml/½ tsp caster (superfine) sugar
    300ml/½ pint/1¼ cups fruity
      white wine
    475ml/16fl oz/2 cups lamb stock or
      half stock and half water
    1 fresh bay leaf
    fresh thyme sprig
    fresh parsley sprig
    500g/1¼lb small new potatoes
    250g/9oz shallots, peeled but
      left whole
    45ml/3 tbsp double (heavy)
      cream (optional)
    salt and ground black pepper
For the gremolata
    1 garlic clove, finely chopped
    finely shredded rind of ½ lemon
    45ml/3 tbsp chopped fresh flat
      leaf parsley

1 Mix the lamb with the garlic and the rind and juice of ½ lemon. Season with pepper and mix in 15ml/1 tbsp olive oil, then leave to marinate for 12–24 hours.

2 Drain the lamb, reserving the marinade, and pat the lamb dry with kitchen paper. Preheat the oven to 180°C/350°F/Gas 4.

COOK'S TIP
A mezzaluna (double-handled, half-moon shaped chopping blade) makes a good job of chopping gremolata ingredients. If using a food processor, take care not to overprocess the mixture as it is easy to mince (grind) it to a paste.

3 Heat 30ml/2 tbsp olive oil in a large, heavy frying pan. Season the flour with salt and pepper and toss the lamb in it to coat, shaking off any excess. Seal the lamb on all sides in the hot oil. Do this in batches, transferring each batch of lamb to an ovenproof pan or flameproof casserole as you brown it. You may need to add an extra 15ml/1 tbsp olive oil to the pan.

4 Reduce the heat, add another 15ml/ 1 tbsp oil to the pan and cook the onion gently over a very low heat, stirring frequently, for 10 minutes, until softened and golden but not browned. Add the anchovies and caster sugar and cook, mashing the anchovies into the soft onion with a wooden spoon.

5 Add the reserved marinade, increase the heat a little and cook for about 1–2 minutes, then pour in the wine and stock or stock and water and bring to the boil. Simmer gently for about 5 minutes, then pour over the lamb.

6 Tie the bay leaf, thyme and parsley together and add to the lamb. Season with salt and pepper, then cover tightly and cook in the oven for 1 hour. Stir the potatoes into the stew and cook for a further 20 minutes.

7 Meanwhile, to make the gremolata, chop all the ingredients together finely. Place in a dish, cover and set aside.

8 Heat the remaining oil in a frying pan and brown the shallots on all sides, then stir them into the lamb. Cover and cook for a further 30–40 minutes, until the lamb is tender. Transfer the lamb and vegetables to a dish and keep warm. Discard the herbs.

9 Boil the cooking juices to reduce and concentrate them, then add the cream, if using, and simmer for 2–3 minutes. Adjust the seasoning, adding a little lemon juice to taste. Pour this sauce over the lamb, sprinkle the gremolata on top and serve immediately.

CALF'S LIVER <u>WITH</u> SLOW-COOKED ONIONS, MARSALA <u>AND</u> SAGE

LIVER AND ONIONS ARE AN INTERNATIONAL FAVOURITE, FROM BRITISH LIVER WITH ONION GRAVY TO THE FAMOUS VENETIAN DISH OF FEGATO ALLA VENEZIANA. INSPIRED BY ITALIAN COOKING, THIS DISH IS GOOD SERVED WITH POLENTA, EITHER SOFT OR SET AND GRILLED.

SERVES FOUR

INGREDIENTS
   45ml/3 tbsp olive oil, plus extra for
     shallow frying
   25g/1oz/2 tbsp butter
   500g/1¼lb mild onions,
     thinly sliced
   small bunch of fresh sage leaves
   30ml/2 tbsp chopped fresh parsley,
     plus a little extra to garnish
   2.5ml/½ tsp caster (superfine) sugar
   15ml/1 tbsp balsamic vinegar
   30ml/2 tbsp plain (all-purpose) flour
   675g/1½lb calf's liver,
     thinly sliced
   150ml/¼ pint/⅔ cup Marsala
   salt and ground black pepper

1 Heat half the olive oil with half the butter in a large, wide, heavy pan and cook the onions, covered, over a very gentle heat for 30 minutes. Stir once or twice during cooking.

2 Chop 5 of the sage leaves and add them to the pan with the parsley, a pinch of salt, the sugar and balsamic vinegar. Cook, uncovered and stirring frequently, until very tender and golden. Taste for seasoning and add salt and pepper as necessary.

3 Heat a shallow layer of olive oil in a frying pan and cook the remaining sage leaves for 15–30 seconds, then drain them on kitchen paper.

4 Heat the remaining butter and oil together in a frying pan over a high heat. Season the flour, then dip the liver in it and cook it quickly for about 2 minutes on each side, until browned, but still pink in the middle. Use a slotted spoon to transfer the liver to warm plates and keep warm.

5 Immediately add the Marsala to the pan and let it bubble fiercely until reduced to a few tablespoons of sticky glaze. Distribute the onions over the liver and spoon over the Marsala juices. Sprinkle with the fried sage leaves and extra parsley and serve immediately.

VARIATION
Chicken liver and onion bruschetta Cook the onions as above, replacing the sage with 5ml/1 tsp chopped thyme. Cook 400g/14oz trimmed chicken livers in 25g/1oz/2 tbsp butter and 15ml/1 tbsp oil until browned but still pink in the centre. Flame the chicken livers with 45ml/3 tbsp Cognac, and add 150g/ 5oz seeded, skinned grapes (optional). Heat the grapes through, then toss into the cooked onions. Heap on to thick slices of toasted country bread rubbed with oil and garlic or on to slices of grilled polenta. Serve sprinkled with chopped fresh parsley.

BEEF CARBONADE

THIS RICH, DARK STEW OF BEEF COOKED SLOWLY WITH LOTS OF ONIONS, GARLIC AND BEER IS A CLASSIC CASSEROLE FROM THE NORTH OF FRANCE AND NEIGHBOURING BELGIUM.

3 Reduce the heat and return the onions to the pan. Add the garlic, cook briefly, then add the beer or ale, water and sugar. Tie the thyme and bay leaf together and add to the pan with the celery. Bring to the boil, stirring, then season with salt and pepper.

4 Pour the sauce over the beef and mix well. Cover tightly, then place in the oven for 2½ hours. Check the beef once or twice to make sure that it is not too dry, adding a little water if necessary. Test for tenderness, allowing an extra 30–40 minutes' cooking if necessary.

SERVES SIX

INGREDIENTS
    45ml/3 tbsp vegetable oil or
      beef dripping
    3 onions, sliced
    45ml/3 tbsp plain (all-purpose) flour
    2.5ml/½ tsp mustard powder
    1kg/2¼lb stewing beef, such as shin
      (shank) or chuck, cut into cubes
    2–3 garlic cloves, finely chopped
    300ml/½ pint/1¼ cups dark beer or ale
    150ml/¼ pint/⅔ cup water
    5ml/1 tsp dark brown sugar
    1 fresh thyme sprig
    1 fresh bay leaf
    1 piece of celery stick
    salt and ground black pepper
For the topping
    50g/2oz/½ cup butter
    1 garlic clove, crushed
    15ml/1 tbsp Dijon mustard
    45ml/3 tbsp chopped fresh parsley
    6–12 slices baguette or ficelle loaf

1 Preheat the oven to 160°C/325°F/ Gas 3. Heat 30ml/2 tbsp of the oil or dripping in a frying pan and cook the onions over a low heat until softened. Remove from the pan and set aside.

2 Meanwhile, mix together the flour and mustard and season. Toss the beef in the flour. Add the remaining oil or dripping to the pan and heat over a high heat. Brown the beef all over, then transfer it to a casserole.

5 To make the topping, cream the butter with the garlic, mustard and 30ml/2 tbsp of the parsley. Spread the butter thickly over the bread. Increase the oven temperature to 190°C/375°F/ Gas 5. Taste and season the casserole, then arrange the bread slices, buttered side uppermost, on top. Bake for 20–25 minutes, until the bread is browned and crisp. Sprinkle the remaining parsley over the top and serve immediately.

VEAL ᴵᴺ A WHEAT BEER SAUCE ᵂᴵᵀᴴ ONIONS ᴬᴺᴰ CARROTS

WHEAT BEERS ARE MADE IN BAVARIA, BELGIUM AND NORTHERN FRANCE, WHERE THEY ARE KNOWN AS BIÈRES BLANCHES OR WHITE BEERS. THE SLIGHT BITTERNESS THAT THE BEER GIVES THE SAUCE IN THIS DELECTABLE STEW IS MATCHED BY THE SWEETNESS OF THE CARAMELIZED ONIONS AND CARROTS.

SERVES FOUR

INGREDIENTS
45ml/3 tbsp plain (all-purpose) flour
900g/2lb boned shoulder or leg of
  veal, cut into 5cm/2in cubes
65g/2½oz/5 tbsp butter
3 shallots, finely chopped
1 celery stick
fresh parsley sprig
2 fresh bay leaves
5ml/1 tsp caster (superfine) sugar,
  plus a good pinch
200ml/7fl oz/scant 1 cup wheat beer
450ml/¾ pint/scant 2 cups
  veal stock
20–25 large silverskin onions or
  small pickling onions
450g/1lb carrots, thickly sliced
2 large (US extra large) egg yolks
105ml/7 tbsp double (heavy) cream
a little lemon juice (optional)
30ml/2 tbsp chopped fresh parsley
salt and ground black pepper

1 Season the flour and dust the veal with it. Heat 25g/1oz/2 tbsp of the butter in a deep, lidded frying pan, add the veal and quickly seal it on all sides. The veal should be golden but not dark brown. Use a slotted spoon to remove the veal from the pan and set aside.

2 Reduce the heat, add another 15g/½oz/1 tbsp butter to the pan and cook the shallots gently for 5–6 minutes, until soft and yellow.

3 Replace the veal. Tie the celery, parsley and 1 bay leaf together in a bundle, then add them to the pan with a good pinch of caster sugar. Increase the heat, pour in the beer and allow to bubble briefly before pouring in the stock. Season, bring to the boil, then cover and simmer gently, stirring once or twice, for 40–50 minutes, or until the veal is cooked and tender.

4 Meanwhile, melt the remaining butter in another frying pan and add the onions, then cook them over a low heat until golden all over. Use a slotted spoon to remove the onions from the pan and set aside.

5 Add the carrots and turn to coat them in the butter remaining from the onions. Stir in 5ml/1 tsp caster sugar, a pinch of salt, the remaining bay leaf and enough water to cover the carrots. Bring to the boil and cook, uncovered, for 10–12 minutes.

6 Return the onions to the pan with the carrots and continue to cook until all but a few tablespoons of the liquid has evaporated and the onions and carrots are tender and slightly caramelized. Keep warm.

7 Use a slotted spoon to transfer the veal to a bowl and discard the celery and herb bundle.

8 Beat the egg yolks and cream together in another bowl, then beat in a ladleful of the hot, but not boiling, carrot liquid. Return this mixture to the pan and cook over a very low heat without boiling, stirring constantly, until the sauce has thickened a little.

9 Add the veal to the sauce, add the onions and carrots and reheat gently until thoroughly warmed through. Taste and adjust the seasoning, adding a little lemon juice, if necessary, then serve immediately, sprinkled with the parsley.

Apart from those vegetarians whose religious beliefs forbid the eating of alliums, onions are an essential part of meat-free cookery around the globe. From the strongest garlic to the mildest chives, all the members of the onion family are delicious with eggs, cheese and dairy foods. Favourites such as Red Onion Tart with a Cornmeal Crust, Frittata with Leek, Red Pepper and Spinach or Three Allium Risotto would be unimaginable without onions. Here is a selection of meat-free dishes that shows just how essential onions really are.

Vegetarian
Main Meals

CHEESE AND LEEK SAUSAGES WITH TOMATO, GARLIC AND CHILLI SAUCE

THESE ARE BASED ON THE WELSH SPECIALITY OF GLAMORGAN SAUSAGES, WHICH ARE TRADITIONALLY MADE USING WHITE OR WHOLEMEAL BREADCRUMBS ALONE. HOWEVER, ADDING A LITTLE MASHED POTATO LIGHTENS THE SAUSAGES AND MAKES THEM MUCH EASIER TO HANDLE.

SERVES FOUR

INGREDIENTS
  25g/1oz/2 tbsp butter
  175g/6oz leeks, finely chopped
  90ml/6 tbsp cold mashed potato
  115g/4oz/2 cups fresh white or
    wholemeal (whole-
    wheat) breadcrumbs
  150g/5oz/1¼ cups grated Caerphilly,
    Lancashire or Cantal cheese
  30ml/2 tbsp chopped fresh parsley
  5ml/1 tsp chopped fresh sage
  2 large (US extra large) eggs, beaten
  cayenne pepper
  65g/2½oz/1 cup dry
    white breadcrumbs
  oil, for shallow frying
For the sauce
  30ml/2 tbsp olive oil
  2 garlic cloves, thinly sliced
  1 fresh red chilli, seeded and finely
    chopped, or a good pinch of dried
    red chilli flakes
  1 small onion, finely chopped
  500g/1¼lb tomatoes, peeled, seeded
    and chopped
  few fresh thyme sprigs
  10ml/2 tsp balsamic vinegar or red
    wine vinegar
  pinch of light muscovado
    (brown) sugar
  15–30ml/1–2 tbsp chopped fresh
    marjoram or oregano
  salt and ground black pepper

1 Melt the butter and cook the leeks for 4–5 minutes, until softened but not browned. Mix with the mashed potato, fresh breadcrumbs, cheese, parsley and sage. Add sufficient beaten egg (about two-thirds of the quantity) to bind. Season and add a pinch of cayenne.

COOK'S TIP
These sausages are also delicious served with garlic mayonnaise or a confit of slow-cooked onions.

2 Shape the mixture into 12 sausage shapes. Dip in the remaining egg, then coat with the dry breadcrumbs. Chill the coated sausages.

3 To make the sauce, heat the oil over a low heat in a pan, add the garlic, chilli and onion and cook for 3–4 minutes. Add the tomatoes, thyme and vinegar. Season with salt, pepper and sugar.

4 Cook the sauce for 40–50 minutes, until much reduced. Remove the thyme and process the sauce in a blender. Reheat with the marjoram or oregano, then adjust the seasoning, adding more sugar if necessary.

5 Cook the sausages in shallow oil until golden brown on all sides. Drain on kitchen paper and serve with the sauce.

POTATO AND ONION CAKES
WITH BEETROOT RELISH

THESE IRRESISTIBLE PANCAKES ARE BASED ON TRADITIONAL LATKE (GRATED POTATO CAKES). THEY ARE ESPECIALLY DELICIOUS WITH A SWEET-SHARP BEETROOT RELISH AND SOUR CREAM.

SERVES FOUR

INGREDIENTS
  500g/1¼lb potatoes
  1 small cooking apple, peeled, cored
    and coarsely grated
  1 small onion, finely chopped
  50g/2oz/½ cup plain (all-
    purpose) flour
  2 large (US extra large) eggs, beaten
  30ml/2 tbsp chopped fresh chives
  vegetable oil, for shallow frying
  salt and ground black pepper
  250ml/8fl oz/1 cup sour cream
    or crème fraîche, to serve
  fresh dill sprigs and fresh chives
    or chive flowers, to garnish
For the beetroot relish
  250g/9oz beetroot (beet), cooked
    and peeled
  1 large dessert apple, cored and
    finely diced
  15ml/1 tbsp finely chopped red onion
  15–30ml/1–2 tbsp tarragon vinegar
  15ml/1 tbsp chopped fresh dill
  15–30ml/1–2 tbsp light olive oil
  pinch of caster sugar (optional)

3 Mix the potatoes, apple and onion in a bowl. Stir in the flour, eggs and chopped chives. Season and mix again.

4 Heat about 5mm/¼in depth of oil in a frying pan and fry spoonfuls of the mixture. Flatten them to make pancakes 7.5–10cm/3–4in across and cook for 3–4 minutes on each side, until browned. Drain on kitchen paper and keep warm until the mixture is used up.

5 Serve a stack of hot pancakes – there should be about 16–20 in total – with spoonfuls of sour cream and beetroot relish. Garnish with dill sprigs and fresh chives or chive flowers, and coarsely grind black pepper on top just before serving.

VARIATION
To make a leek and potato cake, melt 25g/1oz/2 tbsp butter in a pan, add 400g/14oz thinly sliced leeks and cook until tender. Season well. Coarsely grate 500g/1¼lb peeled potatoes, then season. Melt another 25g/1oz/2 tbsp butter in a medium frying pan and add a layer of half the potatoes. Cover with the leeks, then add the remaining potatoes, pressing down with a spatula to form a cake. Cook for 20–25 minutes over a low heat until the potatoes are browned, then turn over and cook for 15–20 minutes, until the potatoes are browned.

1 To make the relish, finely dice the beetroot, then mix it with the apple and onion. Add 15ml/1 tbsp of the vinegar, the dill and 15ml/1 tbsp of the oil. Season, adding more vinegar and oil, and a pinch of caster sugar to taste.

2 Coarsely grate the potatoes, then rinse in cold water, drain and dry them on a clean dishtowel.

PEPPERS FILLED <u>WITH</u> SPICED VEGETABLES

INDIAN SPICES SEASON THE POTATO AND AUBERGINE STUFFING IN THESE COLOURFUL BAKED PEPPERS. THEY ARE GOOD WITH PLAIN RICE AND A LENTIL DHAL. ALTERNATIVELY, SERVE THEM WITH A SALAD, INDIAN BREADS AND A CUCUMBER OR MINT AND YOGURT RAITA.

SERVES SIX

INGREDIENTS

6 large evenly shaped red or
   yellow (bell) peppers
500g/1¼lb waxy potatoes
1 small onion, chopped
4–5 garlic cloves, chopped
5cm/2in piece of fresh root
   ginger, chopped
1–2 fresh green chillies, seeded
   and chopped
105ml/7 tbsp water
90–105ml/6–7 tbsp groundnut
   (peanut) oil
1 aubergine (eggplant), diced
10ml/2 tsp cumin seeds
5ml/1 tsp kalonji seeds
2.5ml/½ tsp ground turmeric
5ml/1 tsp ground coriander
5ml/1 tsp ground toasted
   cumin seeds
pinch of cayenne pepper
about 30ml/2 tbsp lemon juice
salt and ground black pepper
30ml/2 tbsp chopped fresh coriander
   (cilantro), to garnish

1 Cut the tops off the red or yellow peppers then remove and discard the seeds. Cut a thin slice off the base of the peppers, if necessary, to make them stand upright.

2 Bring a large pan of lightly salted water to the boil. Add the peppers to the pan and cook for 5–6 minutes. Drain and leave the peppers upside down in a colander.

3 Cook the potatoes in salted, boiling water for 10–12 minutes, until just tender. Drain, cool and peel, then cut into 1cm/½in dice.

4 Put the onion, garlic, ginger and green chillies in a food processor or blender with 60ml/4 tbsp of the water and process to a purée.

5 Heat 45ml/3 tbsp of the oil in a large, deep frying pan and cook the aubergine, stirring occasionally, until browned on all sides. Remove from the pan and set aside. Add another 30ml/ 2 tbsp of the oil to the pan and cook the potatoes until lightly browned. Remove from the pan and set aside.

6 If necessary, add another 15ml/ 1 tbsp oil to the pan, then add the cumin and kalonji seeds. Cook briefly until they darken, then add the turmeric, coriander and ground cumin. Cook for 15 seconds. Stir in the onion and garlic purée and cook, scraping the pan with a spatula, until it begins to brown.

7 Return the potatoes and aubergines to the pan, season with salt, pepper and 1–2 pinches of cayenne. Add the remaining water and 15ml/1 tbsp lemon juice and then cook, stirring, until the liquid evaporates. Preheat the oven to 190°C/375°F/Gas 5.

8 Fill the peppers with the potato mixture and place on a lightly greased baking tray. Brush the peppers with a little oil and bake for 30–35 minutes, until the peppers are cooked. Leave to cool slightly, then sprinkle with a little more lemon juice, garnish with the coriander and serve.

COOK'S TIP
Kalonji, or nigella as it is sometimes known, is a tiny black seed. It is widely used in Indian cookery, especially sprinkled over breads or in potato dishes. It has a mild, slightly nutty flavour and is best toasted for a few seconds in a dry frying pan over a medium heat. This helps to bring out its flavour.

ONIONS STUFFED <u>WITH</u> GOAT'S CHEESE <u>AND</u> SUN-DRIED TOMATOES

ROASTED ONIONS AND GOAT'S CHEESE ARE A WINNING COMBINATION. THESE STUFFED ONIONS MAKE AN EXCELLENT MAIN COURSE WHEN SERVED WITH A RICE OR CRACKED WHEAT PILAFF.

<u>SERVES FOUR</u>

INGREDIENTS

    4 large onions
    150g/5oz goat's cheese, crumbled
      or cubed
    50g/2oz/1 cup fresh breadcrumbs
    8 sun-dried tomatoes in olive oil,
      drained and chopped
    1–2 garlic cloves, finely chopped
    2.5ml/½ tsp chopped fresh thyme
    30ml/2 tbsp chopped fresh parsley
    1 small (US medium) egg, beaten
    45ml/3 tbsp pine nuts, toasted
    30ml/2 tbsp olive oil (use oil from
      the tomatoes)
    salt and ground black pepper

1 Bring a large pan of lightly salted water to the boil. Add the whole onions in their skins and boil for 10 minutes. Drain and cool, then cut each onion in half horizontally and peel.

2 Using a teaspoon, remove the centre of each onion, leaving a thick shell. Reserve the flesh and place the shells in an oiled ovenproof dish. Preheat the oven to 190°C/375°F/Gas 5.

3 Chop the scooped-out onion flesh and place in a bowl. Add the goat's cheese, breadcrumbs, sun-dried tomatoes, garlic, thyme, parsley and egg. Mix well, then season with salt and pepper and add the toasted pine nuts.

4 Divide the stuffing among the onions and cover with foil. Bake for about 25 minutes. Uncover, drizzle with the oil and cook for another 30–40 minutes, until bubbling and well cooked. Baste occasionally during cooking.

VARIATIONS
• Use feta cheese in place of the goat's cheese and substitute chopped mint, currants and pitted black olives for the other flavourings.
• Stuff the onions with spinach and rice mixed with some smoked mozzarella and toasted almonds instead of the goat's cheese and sun-dried tomato mixture.
• Use red and yellow (bell) peppers preserved in oil instead of tomatoes.
• Substitute 175g/6oz Roquefort or Gorgonzola for the goat's cheese, omit the sun-dried tomatoes and pine nuts, and add 75g/3oz/¾ cup chopped walnuts and 115g/4oz/1 cup chopped celery, cooked until soft with the chopped onion in 25ml/1½ tbsp olive oil.

RED ONION TART <u>WITH</u> A CORNMEAL CRUST

RED ONIONS ARE WONDERFULLY MILD AND SWEET WHEN COOKED AND THEY GO WELL WITH FONTINA CHEESE AND THYME IN THIS TART. CORNMEAL GIVES THE PASTRY A CRUMBLY TEXTURE TO CONTRAST WITH THE JUICINESS OF THE ONION FILLING. A TOMATO AND BASIL SALAD IS GOOD WITH THE TART.

SERVES FIVE TO SIX

INGREDIENTS
  60ml/4 tbsp olive oil
  1kg/2¼lb red onions, thinly sliced
  2–3 garlic cloves, thinly sliced
  5ml/1 tsp chopped fresh thyme, plus
   a few whole sprigs
  5ml/1 tsp dark brown sugar
  10ml/2 tsp sherry vinegar
  225g/8oz fontina cheese, sliced
  salt and ground black pepper
For the pastry
  115g/4oz/1 cup plain
   (all-purpose) flour
  75g/3oz/¾ cup fine yellow cornmeal
  5ml/1 tsp dark brown sugar
  5ml/1 tsp chopped fresh thyme
  90g/3½oz/7 tbsp butter
  1 egg yolk
  30–45ml/2–3 tbsp iced water

1 To make the pastry, sift the plain flour and cornmeal into a bowl with 5ml/1 tsp salt. Add plenty of black pepper and stir in the sugar and thyme. Rub in the butter until the mixture looks like breadcrumbs. Beat the egg yolk with 30ml/2 tbsp iced water and use to bind the pastry, adding another 15ml/1 tbsp iced water, if necessary. Gather the dough into a ball, wrap in clear film (plastic wrap) and chill for 30–40 minutes.

2 Heat 45ml/3 tbsp of the oil in a large, deep frying pan and add the onions. Cover and cook over a low heat, stirring occasionally, for 20–30 minutes. They should collapse but not brown.

3 Add the garlic and chopped thyme, then cook, stirring occasionally, for another 10 minutes. Increase the heat slightly, then add the sugar and sherry vinegar. Cook, uncovered, for a further 5–6 minutes, until the onions start to caramelize slightly. Season to taste with salt and pepper. Cool.

4 Preheat the oven to 190°C/375°F/ Gas 5. Roll out the pastry thinly and use to line a 25cm/10in loose-based metal flan tin (quiche pan).

5 Prick the pastry all over with a fork and support the sides with foil. Bake for 12–15 minutes, until lightly coloured.

6 Remove the foil and spread the onions evenly over the base of the pastry case (pie shell). Add the slices of fontina and thyme sprigs and season with pepper. Drizzle over the remaining oil, then bake for 15–20 minutes, until the filling is piping hot and the cheese is beginning to bubble. Garnish the tart with thyme and serve immediately.

SHALLOT AND GARLIC TARTE TATIN WITH PARMESAN PASTRY

SAVOURY VERSIONS OF THE FAMOUS APPLE TARTE TATIN HAVE BEEN POPULAR FOR SOME YEARS. HERE, SHALLOTS ARE CARAMELIZED IN BUTTER, SUGAR AND VINEGAR BEFORE BEING BAKED BENEATH A LAYER OF PARMESAN PASTRY. THIS IS DELICIOUS SERVED WITH A PEAR, CHEESE AND WATERCRESS SALAD.

2 Melt the butter in a 23–25cm/9–10in round heavy tin (pan) or frying pan that will go in the oven. Add the shallots and garlic and cook until lightly browned.

3 Sprinkle the sugar over the top and increase the heat a little. Cook until the sugar begins to caramelize, then turn the shallots and garlic in the buttery juices. Add the vinegar, water, thyme and seasoning. Cook, part-covered, for 5–8 minutes, until the garlic cloves are just tender. Cool.

SERVES FOUR TO SIX

INGREDIENTS
   300g/11oz puff pastry, thawed
     if frozen
   50g/2oz/¼ cup butter
   75g/3oz/1 cup freshly grated
   Parmesan cheese
For the topping
   40g/1½oz/3 tbsp butter
   500g/1¼lb shallots
   12–16 large garlic cloves, peeled but
     left whole
   15ml/1 tbsp golden caster
     (superfine) sugar
   15ml/1 tbsp balsamic vinegar
   45ml/3 tbsp water
   5ml/1 tsp chopped fresh thyme, plus
     a few extra sprigs (optional)
   salt and ground black pepper

1 Roll out the pastry into a rectangle. Spread the butter over it, leaving a 2.5cm/1in border. Sprinkle the cheese on top. Fold the bottom third of the pastry up to cover the middle and the top third down. Seal the edges, give a quarter turn and roll out to a rectangle, then fold as before. Chill for 30 minutes.

4 Preheat the oven to 190°C/375°F/ Gas 5. Roll out the pastry to the diameter of the tin or frying pan and lay it over the shallots and garlic, tucking it in. Prick the pastry with a sharp knife, then bake for 25–35 minutes, or until the pastry is risen and golden. Set aside to cool for 5–10 minutes, then invert the tart on to a serving platter. Sprinkle with a few thyme sprigs, if you like, and serve immediately.

FRITTATA <u>WITH</u> LEEK, RED PEPPER <u>AND</u> SPINACH

APART FROM THE FACT THAT ITALIAN FRITTATA DOES NOT USUALLY CONTAIN POTATO AND IS GENERALLY SLIGHTLY SOFTER IN TEXTURE, IT IS NOT HUGELY DIFFERENT FROM SPANISH TORTILLA. THIS COMBINATION OF SWEET LEEK, RED PEPPER AND SPINACH IS DELICIOUS WITH THE EGG.

SERVES THREE TO FOUR

INGREDIENTS
  30ml/2 tbsp olive oil
  1 large red (bell) pepper, seeded
    and diced
  2.5–5ml/½–1 tsp ground
    toasted cumin
  3 leeks (about 450g/1lb),
    thinly sliced
  150g/5oz small spinach leaves
  45ml/3 tbsp pine nuts, toasted
  5 large (US extra large) eggs
  15ml/1 tbsp chopped fresh basil
  15ml/1 tbsp chopped fresh flat
    leaf parsley
  salt and ground black pepper
  watercress, to garnish
  50g/2oz Parmesan cheese, grated,
    to serve (optional)

1 Heat a frying pan and add the oil. Add the red pepper and cook over a medium heat, stirring occasionally, for 6–8 minutes, until soft and beginning to brown. Add 2.5ml/½ tsp of the cumin and cook for another 1–2 minutes.

2 Stir in the leeks, then part-cover the pan and cook gently for about 5 minutes, until the leeks have softened and collapsed. Season well.

3 Add the spinach and cover. Allow the spinach to wilt in the steam for 3–4 minutes, then stir to mix it into the vegetables, adding the pine nuts.

4 Beat the eggs with salt, pepper, the remaining cumin, basil and parsley. Add to the pan and cook over a gentle heat until the base of the omelette sets and turns golden brown. Pull the edges of the omelette away from the sides of the pan as it cooks and tilt the pan so that the uncooked egg runs underneath.

5 Preheat the grill (broiler). Flash the frittata under the hot grill to set the egg on top, but do not let it become too brown. Cut the frittata into wedges and serve warm, garnished with watercress and sprinkled with Parmesan, if using.

VARIATION
A delicious way to serve frittata is to pack it into a slightly hollowed-out loaf and then drizzle it with a little extra virgin olive oil. Wrap tightly in clear film (plastic wrap) and leave to stand for 1–2 hours before slicing thickly. A frittata-filled loaf is ideal picnic fare.

ROASTED GARLIC AND AUBERGINE CUSTARDS WITH RED PEPPER DRESSING

THESE ELEGANT LITTLE MOULDS MAKE A RATHER SPLENDID MAIN COURSE FOR A SPECIAL DINNER.
SERVE GOOD BREAD AND STEAMED BROCCOLI AS ACCOMPANIMENTS.

SERVES SIX

INGREDIENTS
    2 large heads of garlic
    6–7 fresh thyme sprigs
    60ml/4 tbsp extra virgin olive oil,
       plus extra for greasing
    350g/12oz aubergines (eggplant), cut
       into 1cm/½in dice
    2 large red (bell) peppers, halved
       and seeded
    pinch of saffron threads
    300ml/½ pint/1¼ cups
       whipping cream
    2 large (US extra large) eggs
    pinch of caster (superfine) sugar
    30ml/2 tbsp shredded fresh
       basil leaves
    salt and ground black pepper
For the dressing
    90ml/6 tbsp extra virgin oil
    15–25ml/1–1½ tbsp balsamic vinegar
    pinch of caster sugar
    115g/4oz tomatoes, peeled, seeded
       and finely diced
    ½ small red onion, finely chopped
    generous pinch of ground toasted
       cumin seeds
    handful of fresh basil leaves

1 Preheat the oven to 190°C/375°F/
Gas 5. Place the garlic on a piece of foil
with the thyme and sprinkle with 15ml/
1 tbsp of the oil. Wrap the foil around
the garlic and cook for 35–45 minutes,
or until the garlic is soft. Cool slightly.
Reduce the oven temperature to 180°C/
350°F/Gas 4.

2 Meanwhile, heat the remaining olive
oil in a large, heavy pan. Add the diced
aubergines and cook over a medium
heat, stirring frequently, for about
5–8 minutes, until they are browned
and cooked.

3 Grill (broil) the peppers, skin sides
uppermost, until they are black. Place
the peppers in a bowl, cover and leave
for 10 minutes.

4 When the peppers are cool enough to
handle, peel and dice them. Soak the
saffron in 15ml/1 tbsp hot water for
10 minutes.

5 Unwrap the roasted garlic and pop
the cloves out of their skins into a
blender or food processor. Discard the
thyme sprigs. Add the oil from cooking,
the cream and eggs to the garlic.
Process until smooth. Add the soaked
saffron with its liquid and season well
with salt, pepper and a pinch of sugar.
Stir in half the diced red pepper and
the basil.

6 Lightly grease six large ovenproof
ramekins (about 200–250ml/7–8fl oz/
1 cup capacity), lining e the base of
each with non-stick baking parchment.

COOK'S TIP
It is important that the custards cook at
an even temperature throughout and are
surround by a water bath or they may
crack, spoiling their appearance.

7 Divide the aubergines among the
dishes. Pour the egg mixture into
the ramekins, then place them in a
roasting pan. Cover each dish with foil
and make a little hole in the centre of
the foil to allow steam to escape. Pour
hot water into the pan to come halfway
up the outsides of the ramekins. Bake
for 25–30 minutes, until the custards
are just set in the centre.

8 Make the dressing while the custards
are cooking. Whisk the oil and vinegar
with salt, pepper and a pinch of
sugar. Stir in the tomatoes, red onion,
remaining red pepper and cumin.
Set aside some basil leaves for
garnishing, then chop the rest and
add to the dressing.

9 Leave the custards to cool for about
5 minutes, then turn them out on to
warmed serving plates. Spoon the
dressing around the custards and
garnish each with the reserved fresh
basil leaves.

PASTA WITH PESTO, POTATOES AND GREEN BEANS

THIS IS ONE OF THE TRADITIONAL WAYS TO SERVE PESTO IN LIGURIA. ALTHOUGH THE COMBINATION OF PASTA AND POTATOES MAY SEEM ODD, IT IS DELICIOUS WITH THE RICH PESTO SAUCE.

SERVES FOUR

INGREDIENTS
  50g/2oz/½ cup pine nuts
  2 large garlic cloves, chopped
  90g/3½oz fresh basil leaves, plus a
    few extra leaves
  90ml/6 tbsp extra virgin olive oil (use
    a mild Ligurian or French oil)
  50g/2oz/⅔ cup freshly grated
    Parmesan cheese
  40g/1½oz/½ cup freshly grated
    pecorino cheese
For the pasta mixture
  275g/10oz waxy potatoes, thickly
    sliced or cut into 1cm/½in cubes
  200g/7oz fine green beans
  350g/12oz dried trenette, linguine,
    tagliatelle or tagliarini
  salt and ground black pepper
To serve
  extra virgin olive oil
  pine nuts, toasted
  Parmesan cheese, grated

1 Toast the pine nuts in a dry frying pan until golden. (Watch them carefully or they will burn.) Place in a mortar with the garlic and a pinch of salt, and crush with a pestle. Add the basil and continue pounding the mixture. Gradually add a little oil as you work the mixture to form a paste. Then work in the Parmesan and pecorino with the remaining oil. (Alternatively, blend the pine nuts, garlic, basil and oil in a food processor, then stir in the cheeses.)

2 Bring a pan of lightly salted water to the boil and add the potatoes. Cook for 10–12 minutes, until tender. Add the green beans to the pan for the last 5–6 minutes of the cooking time.

3 Meanwhile, cook the pasta in salted, boiling water for 8–12 minutes, or according to the packet instructions, until just tender. Times vary according to the pasta shapes. Try to time the cooking so that both pasta and potatoes are ready at the same time.

4 Drain the pasta and potatoes and beans. Place in a large, warmed bowl and toss with two-thirds of the pesto. Season with black pepper and sprinkle extra basil leaves over the top.

5 Serve immediately with the rest of the pesto, extra olive oil, pine nuts and grated Parmesan.

COOK'S TIP
To freeze pesto, make it without the cheeses, then freeze. To use, remove the pesto from the freezer and leave to thaw, then simply stir in the cheeses. If you plan to freeze pesto for more than a few weeks, omit the garlic as well and stir it in with the cheeses on thawing, as the flavour of garlic can change during prolonged freezing.

AUBERGINE AND SWEET POTATO STEW WITH GARLIC AND COCONUT MILK

INSPIRED BY THAI COOKING, THIS AUBERGINE AND SWEET POTATO STEW COOKED IN A COCONUT SAUCE IS SCENTED WITH FRAGRANT LEMON GRASS, GINGER AND LOTS OF GARLIC.

SERVES SIX

INGREDIENTS
  60ml/4 tbsp groundnut (peanut) oil
  400g/14oz baby aubergines
    (eggplant), halved, or 2 standard
    aubergines (eggplant), cut
    into chunks
  225g/8oz Thai red shallots or other
    small shallots or pickling onions
  5ml/1 tsp fennel seeds,
    lightly crushed
  4–5 garlic cloves, thinly sliced
  25ml/1½ tbsp finely chopped fresh
    root ginger
  475ml/16fl oz/2 cups vegetable stock
  2 lemon grass stalks, outer layers
    discarded, finely chopped
  15g/½oz/½ cup fresh coriander
    (cilantro), stalks and leaves
    chopped separately
  3 kaffir lime leaves, lightly bruised
  2–3 small red chillies
  45–60ml/3–4 tbsp Thai green
    curry paste
  675g/1½lb sweet potatoes, peeled
    and cut into thick chunks
  400ml/14fl oz/1⅔ cups coconut milk
  2.5–5ml/½–1 tsp light muscovado
    (brown) sugar
  250g/9oz mushrooms, thickly sliced
  juice of 1 lime, to taste
  salt and ground black pepper
  18 fresh Thai basil leaves or ordinary
    basil, to serve

1 Heat half the oil in a wide pan. Add the aubergines and cook over a medium heat, stirring occasionally, until lightly browned. Remove from the pan.

2 Slice 4–5 of the shallots and set aside. Cook the remaining whole shallots in the oil remaining in the pan, adding a little more oil if necessary, until lightly browned. Set aside with the aubergines. Add the remaining oil to the pan and cook the sliced shallots, fennel seeds, garlic and ginger very gently until soft but not browned.

3 Add the vegetable stock, lemon grass, chopped coriander stalks and any roots, lime leaves and whole chillies. Cover and simmer over a low heat for 5 minutes.

4 Stir in 30ml/2 tbsp of the curry paste and the sweet potatoes. Simmer gently for about 10 minutes, then return the aubergines and browned shallots to the pan and cook for a further 5 minutes.

5 Stir in the coconut milk and the sugar. Season to taste, then stir in the mushrooms and simmer for 5 minutes, or until all the vegetables are cooked.

6 Stir in more curry paste and lime juice to taste, followed by the chopped coriander leaves. Adjust the seasoning and ladle the vegetables into warmed bowls. Sprinkle basil leaves over the vegetables and serve.

PARSNIPS AND CHICKPEAS IN GARLIC, ONION, CHILLI AND GINGER PASTE

THE SWEET FLAVOUR OF PARSNIPS GOES VERY WELL WITH THE SPICES IN THIS INDIAN-STYLE VEGETABLE STEW. OFFER INDIAN BREADS TO MOP UP THE DELICIOUS SAUCE.

SERVES FOUR

INGREDIENTS
   200g/7oz dried chickpeas,
      soaked overnight in cold water,
      then drained
   7 garlic cloves, finely chopped
   1 small onion, chopped
   5cm/2in piece of fresh root
      ginger, chopped
   2 green chillies, seeded and
      finely chopped
   450ml/¾ pint/scant 2 cups plus
      75ml/5 tbsp water
   60ml/4 tbsp groundnut (peanut) oil
   5ml/1 tsp cumin seeds
   10ml/2 tsp ground coriander seeds
   5ml/1 tsp ground turmeric
   2.5–5ml/½–1 tsp chilli powder or
      mild paprika
   50g/2oz cashew nuts, toasted
      and ground
   250g/9oz tomatoes, peeled
      and chopped
   900g/2lb parsnips, cut
      into chunks
   5ml/1 tsp ground toasted
      cumin seeds
   juice of 1 lime, to taste
   salt and ground black pepper
To serve
   fresh coriander (cilantro) leaves
   a few cashew nuts, toasted

1 Put the soaked chickpeas in a pan, cover with cold water and bring to the boil. Boil vigorously for 10 minutes, then reduce the heat so that the water boils steadily and cook for 1–1½ hours, or until the chickpeas are tender. (The exact cooking time depends on how long the chickpeas have been stored.) Drain thoroughly.

2 Set 10ml/2 tsp of the garlic aside, then place the remainder in a food processor or blender with the onion, ginger and half the chillies. Add the 75ml/5 tbsp water and process to make a smooth paste.

3 Heat the oil in a large, deep, frying pan and cook the cumin seeds for 30 seconds. Stir in the coriander seeds, turmeric, chilli powder or paprika and the ground cashew nuts. Add the ginger and chilli paste and cook, stirring frequently, until the water begins to evaporate. Add the tomatoes and stir-fry until the mixture begins to turn red-brown in colour.

4 Mix in the chickpeas and parsnips with the main batch of water, 5ml/1 tsp salt and plenty of black pepper. Bring to the boil, stir, then simmer, uncovered, for 15–20 minutes, until the parsnips are completely tender.

5 Reduce the liquid, if necessary, by boiling fiercely until the sauce is thick. Add the ground toasted cumin with more salt and/or lime juice to taste. Stir in the reserved garlic and green chilli, and cook for a further 1–2 minutes. Sprinkle the fresh coriander leaves and toasted cashew nuts over to garnish and serve immediately.

COOK'S TIP
Do not add salt to the water when cooking dried chickpeas, as this will toughen them.

VEGETABLE STEW WITH ROASTED TOMATO AND GARLIC SAUCE

THIS LIGHTLY SPICED STEW MAKES A PERFECT MATCH FOR COUSCOUS ENRICHED WITH A LITTLE BUTTER OR OLIVE OIL. ADD SOME CHOPPED FRESH CORIANDER AND A HANDFUL EACH OF RAISINS AND TOASTED PINE NUTS TO THE COUSCOUS TO MAKE IT EXTRA SPECIAL.

SERVES SIX

INGREDIENTS

45ml/3 tbsp olive oil
250g/9oz small pickling onions
  or shallots
1 large onion, chopped
2 garlic cloves, chopped
5ml/1 tsp cumin seeds
5ml/1 tsp ground coriander seeds
5ml/1 tsp paprika
5cm/2in piece of cinnamon stick
2 fresh bay leaves
300–450ml/½–¾ pint/
  1¼–scant 2 cups good
  vegetable stock
good pinch of saffron threads
450g/1lb carrots, thickly sliced
2 green (bell) peppers, seeded and
  thickly sliced
115g/4oz ready-to-eat dried apricots,
  halved if large
5–7.5ml/1–1½ tsp ground toasted
  cumin seeds
450g/1lb squash, peeled, seeded
  and cut into chunks
pinch of sugar, to taste
25g/1oz/2 tbsp butter (optional)
salt and ground black pepper
45ml/3 tbsp fresh coriander (cilantro)
  leaves, to garnish
For the roasted tomato and garlic sauce
1kg/2¼lb tomatoes, halved
5ml/1 tsp sugar
45ml/3 tbsp olive oil
1–2 fresh red chillies, seeded
  and chopped
2–3 garlic cloves, chopped
5ml/1 tsp fresh thyme leaves

VARIATION

A mixture of aubergine (eggplant) and potato is also good. Cook the cubed aubergine with the shallots until brown and cook the potatoes as you would the squash. Allow 2 medium aubergines and about 500g/1¼lb small potatoes. Omit the carrots and apricots.

1 Preheat the oven to 180°C/350°F/ Gas 4. First make the sauce. Place the tomatoes, cut sides uppermost, in a roasting pan. Season well with salt and pepper and sprinkle the sugar over the top, then drizzle with the olive oil. Roast for 30 minutes.

2 Sprinkle the chillies, garlic and thyme over the tomatoes, stir to mix and roast for another 30–45 minutes, until the tomatoes are collapsed but still a little juicy. Cool, then process in a food processor or blender to make a thick sauce. Sieve to remove the seeds.

3 Heat 30ml/2 tbsp of the oil in a large, wide pan or deep frying pan and cook the pickling onions or shallots until browned all over. Remove from the pan and set aside. Add the chopped onion to the pan and cook over a low heat for 5–7 minutes, until softened. Stir in the garlic and cumin seeds and cook for a further 3–4 minutes.

4 Add the ground coriander seeds, paprika, cinnamon stick and bay leaves. Cook, stirring constantly, for another 2 minutes, then mix in the vegetable stock, saffron, carrots and green peppers. Season well, cover and simmer gently for 10 minutes.

5 Stir in the apricots, 5ml/1 tsp of the ground toasted cumin, the browned onions or shallots and the squash. Stir in the tomato sauce.

6 Cover the pan and cook for a further 5 minutes. Uncover the pan and continue to cook, stirring occasionally, for 10–15 minutes, until the vegetables are all fully cooked.

7 Adjust the seasoning, adding a little more cumin and a pinch of sugar to taste. Remove and discard the cinnamon stick. Stir in the butter, if using, and serve sprinkled with the fresh coriander leaves.

So many sauces, from the classic bases of haute cuisine to

the lively flavoured salsas of modern cooking, rely on the

alliums. Shallots are wonderful in sauces and pickles,

adding a strength of flavour without the bulk of an onion.

Strong-flavoured onions, shallots and garlic are favourites

for pickling across the globe, from the European Pickled

Mushrooms with Garlic and Red Onions, to Hot Thai

Pickled Shallots.

Sauces, Pickles and Pastes

OLD ENGLISH BREAD SAUCE

A CLASSIC SAUCE FOR ROAST GAME, CHICKEN OR TURKEY, BREAD SAUCE IS NOW RESERVED ALMOST EXCLUSIVELY TO ACCOMPANY THE CHRISTMAS TURKEY. HOWEVER, IT IS ALSO GOOD WITH SAUSAGES.

SERVES SIX TO EIGHT

INGREDIENTS
  475ml/16fl oz/2 cups milk
  1 small onion, stuck with 4 cloves
  1 celery stick, chopped
  1 fresh bay leaf, torn in half
  6 allspice berries
  1 mace blade
  90g/3½oz/1¾ cups day-old
    breadcrumbs, from a good-quality
    white loaf
  freshly grated nutmeg
  30ml/2 tbsp double (heavy) cream
  15g/½oz/1 tbsp butter
  salt and ground black pepper

1 Place the milk, onion, celery, bay leaf, allspice and mace in a pan and bring to the boil. Take off the heat, half-cover, and set aside for 30–60 minutes.

2 Strain the milk and place in a blender or food processor. Remove and discard the cloves from the onion and add the onion to the milk with the celery. Process until smooth, then strain the liquid back into the clean pan.

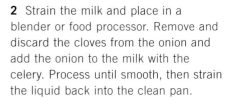

3 Bring back to the boil and stir in the breadcrumbs. Simmer gently, whisking with a small whisk, until the sauce thickens and becomes smooth. Add a little extra milk if the sauce is too thick.

4 Season to taste with salt, pepper and freshly grated nutmeg. Just before serving, whisk in the cream and butter. Serve warm rather than piping hot.

VARIATION
Muhammara, Middle-Eastern bread sauce with peppers and garlic, is good with grilled (broiled) fish or chicken or served as a dip with crudités. Crush 2–3 garlic cloves and place in a food processor or blender with 3 large red (bell) peppers, grilled, skinned and seeded; 1 hot red chilli, grilled, skinned and seeded; 90g/3½oz/scant 1 cup walnuts; and 50g/2oz bread, crusts removed. Process to make a paste, then blend in the juice of half a lemon and 2.5ml/½ tsp each of salt, pepper and muscovado (molasses) sugar. With the motor running, gradually trickle in about 150ml/5fl oz/⅔ cup extra virgin olive oil. Season with more lemon juice, salt, sugar and toasted ground cumin, then stir in 30ml/2 tbsp chopped parsley. Thin the sauce with more oil if necessary.

ONION GRAVY

THIS MAKES A DELICIOUS, DARK ONION SAUCE TO GO WITH SAUSAGES, LIVER OR PORK CHOPS. IT IS ALSO GOOD WITH A MOUND OF CREAMY MASHED POTATOES.

2 Add the sugar, increase the heat slightly and cook for a further 20–30 minutes, until the onions are dark brown.

3 Stir in the flour, cook for a few minutes, stirring constantly, then gradually stir in 400ml/14fl oz/1⅔ cups of the hot stock. Simmer, stirring, to make a thickened gravy, adding a little more stock if the gravy is too thick.

4 Add the thyme, season with a little salt and pepper, then cook very gently, stirring frequently, for 10–15 minutes.

5 Stir in the soy sauce, Worcestershire sauce, if using, and more seasoning, if necessary. Add a little more stock if the gravy is too thick, remove the thyme, and serve immediately.

SERVES FOUR

INGREDIENTS
40g/1½oz/3 tbsp butter or
 beef dripping
450g/1lb onions, halved and
 thinly sliced
2.5ml/½ tsp brown sugar
45ml/3 tbsp plain (all-purpose) flour
400–500ml/14–17fl oz/1⅔–2 cups
 hot beef or vegetable stock
1 fresh thyme sprig
10ml/2 tsp dark soy sauce
5ml/1 tsp Worcestershire
 sauce (optional)
salt and ground black pepper

1 Melt the butter or dripping over a gentle heat. Add the onions and cook, stirring occasionally, for 15–20 minutes, until soft and beginning to brown.

VARIATIONS
• The onions can be browned in the oven. This is best done in vegetable oil rather than butter or dripping. Place the sliced onions in an ovenproof dish and toss with 45ml/3 tbsp oil. Cook at 190°C/375°F/Gas 5 for 20 minutes, stirring once or twice. Stir in the sugar, then cook at 220°C/425°F/Gas 7 for a further 15–25 minutes, until the onions are dark brown and caramelized.
• Part of the beef or vegetable stock may be replaced with red wine or dark beer. You may need to add a little extra sugar to balance the acidity of the wine or beer.

SAUCE SOUBISE

THIS IS THE CLASSIC FRENCH WHITE ONION SAUCE. IT IS EXCELLENT WITH VEAL, CHICKEN, PORK OR LAMB. IT IS ALSO GOOD POURED OVER SLICED HARD-BOILED EGGS OR POACHED EGGS AND THEN GRATINÉED UNDER A HOT GRILL. IT CAN BE LEFT CHUNKY WITH ONION, OR PURÉED.

SERVES FOUR

INGREDIENTS
40g/1½oz/3 tbsp butter
350g/12oz onions, chopped
25g/1oz/¼ cup plain (all-
    purpose) flour
500ml/17fl oz/generous 2 cups hot
    milk or stock, or a mixture of both
1 fresh bay leaf
a few parsley stalks
120ml/4fl oz/½ cup double
    (heavy) cream
freshly grated nutmeg
salt and ground black pepper

1 Melt the butter in a large pan. Cook the onions over a low heat, stirring occasionally, for 10–12 minutes, until soft and golden, but not at all browned.

2 Stir in the flour and cook gently, stirring constantly, for 2–3 minutes.

3 Gradually stir in the hot milk, stock, or milk and stock mixture and bring to the boil. Add the bay leaf and parsley. Part-cover the pan and cook very gently, stirring frequently, for 15–20 minutes.

4 Remove and discard the bay leaf and parsley, then process the sauce in a blender or food processor if you want a smooth sauce.

5 Stir in the cream and reheat the sauce gently, then season to taste with salt and pepper. Add a little more milk or stock if the sauce is very thick. Season with grated nutmeg to taste just before serving.

VARIATIONS
• For leek sauce, substitute leeks for onions, using the white part of the leeks. Cook for just 4–5 minutes in the butter before adding the flour. Omit the nutmeg and stir in 15ml/1 tbsp Dijon mustard just before serving.
• Season the sauce with about 30ml/ 2 tbsp Dijon mustard at the end of cooking to make *sauce Robert* – a classic French sauce traditionally served with pork chops. It also goes very well with ham or rabbit.

COOK'S TIP
The sauce should be cooked for this length of time to cook out the raw flour flavour. A heat diffuser mat is very useful to keep the heat as low as possible when cooking delicate foods.

OLIVE OIL, TOMATO AND HERB SAUCE WITH GARLIC AND SHALLOT

THIS SAUCE IS BASED ON SAUCE VIERGE, A CLASSIC DRESSING USED IN NOUVELLE CUISINE, AND INVENTED BY FRENCH CHEF MICHEL GUÉRARD. IT IS DELICIOUS SERVED WARM, RATHER THAN HOT, WITH GRILLED OR POACHED FISH. SERVE GOOD BREAD OR BOILED NEW POTATOES TO MOP UP THE OIL.

SERVES FOUR TO SIX

INGREDIENTS
    225g/8oz tomatoes
    15ml/1 tbsp finely chopped shallot
    2 garlic cloves, thinly sliced or
      finely chopped
    120ml/4fl oz/½ cup extra virgin
      olive oil
    about 15ml/1 tbsp lemon juice
    caster (superfine) sugar
    15ml/1 tbsp chopped fresh chervil
    15ml/1 tbsp chopped fresh chives
    30ml/2 tbsp torn fresh basil leaves
    salt and ground black pepper

VARIATION
Use diced red (bell) pepper in place of
the tomatoes. Grill (broil), peel, seed and
finely dice the pepper. Use balsamic
vinegar instead of lemon juice and red
onion instead of shallot. Omit the chervil
and use all basil or a mixture of
marjoram and basil. A pinch of ground
toasted cumin seeds is good in this.

1 Peel and seed the tomatoes, then cut
them into fine dice.

2 Place the shallot, garlic and oil in a
small pan over a very gentle heat and
allow to infuse (steep) for a few
minutes. The ingredients should warm
through, but definitely not cook.

COOK'S TIP
It is essential to the flavour of this sauce
that you use the best quality extra virgin
olive oil.

3 Whisk in 30ml/2 tbsp cold water and
10ml/2 tsp lemon juice. Remove from
the heat and stir in the tomatoes. Add a
pinch of salt, pepper and caster sugar,
then whisk in the chervil and chives.

4 Leave the sauce to stand for about
10–15 minutes. Adjust the seasoning,
adding more lemon juice, salt and black
pepper as required.

5 Reheat gently until just warm, then
stir in the basil just before serving.

ROASTED PEPPER AND GARLIC DRESSING

THIS DRESSING IS DELICIOUS ON CHICKEN SALAD OR TOSSED WITH HOT OR COLD PASTA. IT IS ALSO GOOD WITH SALADS OF CHARGRILLED VEGETABLES, PARTICULARLY AUBERGINES AND ONIONS.

SERVES FOUR

INGREDIENTS

2 large heads of garlic, outer skin
   removed but left whole
3 fresh thyme sprigs or 2 fresh
   rosemary sprigs
150ml/¼ pint/⅔ cup olive oil
2 red (bell) peppers, halved
   and seeded
juice of ½ lemon
pinch of caster (superfine) sugar
15ml/1 tbsp chopped fresh chives
   or basil
salt and ground black pepper

COOK'S TIP
If the dressing starts to separate after standing for any length of time, whisk in 15–30ml/1–2 tbsp crème fraîche. This is especially good on hot pasta.

1 Preheat the oven to 190°C/375°F/ Gas 5. Place the garlic on a piece of foil with the herb sprigs and add 15ml/ 1 tbsp of the oil. Close the foil around them and bake for 45–60 minutes, or until the garlic is soft when squeezed. Place the peppers, cut sides down, on a baking sheet and bake at the same time as the garlic, until their skin is blistered.

2 Place the peppers in a bowl, cover and set aside to steam for 10 minutes. Then peel off the skins and place the flesh in a blender or food processor.

3 Set the garlic aside until cool enough to handle, then squeeze the soft pulp out of the skins and into the blender or food processor with the peppers. Add any cooking juices from the foil, but discard the herb sprigs and papery garlic skin, then process the mixture until smooth.

4 Gradually blend in the remaining olive oil while the motor is still running. Gradually add lemon juice to taste. Then season with salt and pepper to taste and add a pinch of sugar. Stir in the chopped chives or basil and use the dressing immediately.

THAI GREEN CURRY PASTE

A FASHIONABLE, FAVOURITE INGREDIENT IN RECENT YEARS, THIS PASTE CAN BE MADE AUTHENTICALLY HOT, OR THE NUMBER OF CHILLIES CAN BE REDUCED FOR A MILDER TASTE.

MAKES ABOUT 120ML/4FL OZ/½ CUP

INGREDIENTS

3 Thai shallots, chopped
3–4 garlic cloves, chopped
4 hot green chillies, seeded, if you
   like, and chopped
2 lemon grass stalks, tender inner
   parts only, chopped
2.5cm/1in piece of fresh galangal
   root or fresh root ginger, chopped
15g/½oz fresh coriander (cilantro),
   with root if possible, chopped
2 kaffir lime leaves
5ml/1 tsp ground toasted
   coriander seeds
2.5ml/½ tsp ground toasted
   cumin seeds
15–25ml/3–5 tsp Thai fish sauce
15–30ml/1–2 tbsp groundnut
   (peanut) oil
pinch of soft light brown sugar
salt and ground black pepper

1 Put the shallots, garlic, chillies, lemon grass, galangal or ginger, fresh coriander, lime leaves, ground coriander and ground cumin in a small food processor or clean coffee grinder. Add fish sauce to taste. Briefly process.

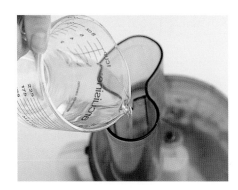

2 Add sufficient groundnut oil to make a paste. Season with salt, pepper and a pinch of sugar. Store for 2–3 days in an air-tight jar in the refrigerator.

VARIATION
To make red curry paste, process 3 thinly sliced shallots, 3–4 chopped garlic cloves, 6–10 seeded bird's eye chillies, 2 chopped lemon grass stalks, 15ml/ 1 tbsp chopped galangal or fresh root ginger, 30ml/2 tbsp chopped coriander (cilantro) root or stalk, 2 kaffir lime leaves and 5ml/1 tsp each toasted coriander seeds, cumin seeds, and paprika, 2.5ml/½ tsp black peppercorns and 5ml/1 tsp shrimp paste. Add the groundnut (peanut) oil and sugar as for the green curry paste. Season to taste with salt. For an authentically hot paste, use a small amount of hot chilli powder in place of the paprika.

Above right: (clockwise from top left) Roasted Red Pepper and Garlic Dressing, Garlic and Rosemary Vinegar, and Thai Green Curry Paste.

GARLIC AND ROSEMARY VINEGAR

Vinegar scented with garlic is useful for flavouring salad dressings instead of adding raw garlic. It is also good for deglazing the pan after cooking poultry or meat.

MAKES 475ML/16FL OZ/2 CUPS

INGREDIENTS
    8–9 large garlic cloves, peeled
    2–3 fresh rosemary sprigs
    1 long fresh rosemary sprig or long
      thin wooden skewer (see method)
    475ml/16fl oz/2 cups good white
      wine vinegar

1 Blanch the garlic and rosemary in boiling water for 30–60 seconds. Drain and pat dry. Strip the leaves from the long rosemary sprig, if using, leaving a few leaves on top. Blanch the stripped sprig or wooden skewer.

2 Thread the garlic cloves on to the stripped sprig or skewer. (This is easier if you sharpen the end of the sprig into a point.)

3 Place the threaded garlic and small rosemary sprigs into a sterilized wide-necked bottle of about 550ml/18fl oz/ 2¼ cup capacity. Heat the vinegar to just below boiling, then carefully pour it into the bottle and cool before sealing. Leave to mature for 3–4 weeks.

VARIATION
You can use other strongly flavoured herbs instead of rosemary, threading the garlic cloves on a thin wooden skewer. Try marjoram, basil or tarragon, for example, or a mixture of fresh herbs. You could also use red wine vinegar instead of white for a variation in flavour.

GARLIC MAYONNAISE

THIS CAN BE AS EASY TO MAKE AS STIRRING CRUSHED GARLIC INTO GOOD QUALITY, READY-MADE MAYONNAISE. BUT A PROPER HOME-MADE MAYONNAISE, WITH GARLIC STIRRED IN, REALLY REVEALS JUST HOW GOOD THIS DELICIOUS DRESSING CAN BE.

SERVES FOUR TO SIX

INGREDIENTS
   2 large (US extra large) egg yolks
   pinch of dried mustard
   up to 300ml/½ pint/1¼ cups mild
      olive oil or olive oil and grapeseed
      oil, mixed
   15–30ml/1–2 tbsp lemon juice,
      white wine vinegar or warm water
   2–4 garlic cloves
   salt and ground black pepper

1 Make sure the egg yolks and oil have come to room temperature before you start. Place the yolks in a bowl with the mustard and a pinch of salt and whisk.

2 Gradually whisk in the oil, one drop at a time. When almost half the oil has been fully incorporated, add it in a steady stream.

3 As the mayonnaise starts to thicken, thin it down with a few drops of lemon juice or vinegar, or a few teaspoons of warm water.

4 When the mayonnaise is as thick as soft butter, stop adding oil. Season the mayonnaise to taste and add more lemon juice or vinegar as required.

WATCHPOINT
The very young, the elderly, pregnant women and those in ill-health or with a compromised immune system are advised against consuming raw eggs or dishes containing raw eggs.

5 Crush the garlic with the blade of a knife and stir it into the mayonnaise. For a slightly milder flavour, blanch the garlic twice in plenty of boiling water, then purée the cloves before beating them into the mayonnaise.

VARIATIONS
• To make Provençal aioli, crush 3–5 garlic cloves with a pinch of salt in a bowl, then whisk in the egg yolks. Omit the mustard but continue as above, using all olive oil.
• For spicy garlic mayonnaise, omit the mustard and stir in 2.5ml/½ tsp harissa or red chilli paste and 5ml/1 tsp sun-dried tomato paste with the garlic.
• Use roasted garlic purée or puréed smoked garlic to create a different flavour.
• Beat in about 15g/½oz mixed fresh herbs such as tarragon, parsley, chervil and chives. Blanch the herbs in boiling water for 20–30 seconds, then drain and pat them dry on kitchen paper before finely chopping them.

PEANUT SAUCE

THIS IS BASED ON THE FAMOUS INDONESIAN SAUCE THAT ACCOMPANIES GRILLED PORK, CHICKEN OR SEAFOOD SATAY. SLIGHTLY THINNED DOWN WITH WATER, IT IS ALSO USED TO DRESS GADO-GADO, A WONDERFUL SALAD OF MIXED RAW OR COOKED VEGETABLES AND FRUIT.

SERVES FOUR TO SIX

INGREDIENTS
30ml/2 tbsp groundnut
   (peanut) oil
75g/3oz/¾ cup unsalted
   peanuts, blanched
2 shallots, chopped
2 garlic cloves, chopped
15ml/1 tbsp chopped fresh
   root ginger
1–2 green chillies, seeded and
   thinly sliced
5ml/1 tsp ground coriander
1 lemon grass stalk, tender base
   only, chopped
5–10ml/1–2 tsp light muscovado
   (brown) sugar
15ml/1 tbsp dark soy sauce
105–120ml/3½–4 fl oz/scant ½ cup
   canned coconut milk
15–30ml/1–2 tbsp Thai fish sauce
15–30ml/1–2 tbsp tamarind purée
lime juice
salt and ground black pepper

3 Transfer the spice mixture to a food processor or blender and add the peanuts, lemon grass, 5ml/1 tsp of the sugar, the soy sauce and 105ml/7 tbsp of coconut milk and the fish sauce. Blend to form a fairly smooth sauce.

4 Taste and add more fish sauce, tamarind purée, seasoning, lime juice and/or more sugar to taste.

COOK'S TIP
To make tamarind purée, soak 25g/1oz tamarind pulp in 120ml/4fl oz/½ cup boiling water in a non-metallic bowl for about 30 minutes, mashing the pulp occasionally with a fork. Then press the pulp through a stainless steel sieve. This purée will keep for several days in a covered container in the refrigerator.

5 Stir in the extra coconut milk and a little water if the sauce seems very thick, but do not let it become runny.

6 Serve cool or reheat the sauce gently, stirring constantly to prevent it from spitting. Garnish with the remaining sliced chilli before serving.

1 Heat the oil in a small, heavy frying pan and gently cook the peanuts, stirring frequently, until lightly browned. Use a slotted spoon to remove the nuts from the pan and drain thoroughly on kitchen paper. Set aside to cool.

2 Add the shallots, garlic, ginger, most of the sliced chillies and the ground coriander to the pan and cook over a low heat, stirring occasionally, for 4–5 minutes, until the shallots are softened but not at all browned.

Coconut Chutney <u>with</u> Onion <u>and</u> Chilli

Serve this refreshing fresh chutney as an accompaniment to Indian-style dishes or with a raita and other chutneys and poppadums at the start of a meal.

SERVES FOUR TO SIX

INGREDIENTS
200g/7oz/2⅓ cups grated
   fresh coconut
3–4 green chillies, seeded
   and chopped
20g/¾oz/¾ cup fresh coriander
   (cilantro), chopped
30ml/2 tbsp chopped fresh mint
30–45ml/2–3 tbsp lime juice
about 2.5ml/½ tsp salt
about 2.5ml/½ tsp caster
   (superfine) sugar
15–30ml/1–2 tbsp coconut
   milk (optional)
30ml/2 tbsp groundnut (peanut) oil
5ml/1 tsp kalonji
1 small onion, very finely chopped
fresh coriander sprigs,
   to garnish

1 Place the coconut, chillies, coriander and mint in a food processor. Add 30ml/2 tbsp of the lime juice, then process until thoroughly chopped.

2 Scrape the mixture into a bowl and add more lime juice to taste. Add salt and sugar to taste. If the mixture is dry, stir in 15–30ml/1–2 tbsp coconut milk.

3 Heat the oil in a small pan and cook the kalonji until they begin to pop, then reduce the heat and add the onion. Cook, stirring frequently, for 4–5 minutes, until the onion softens.

4 Stir the onion mixture into the coconut mixture and leave to cool. Garnish with coriander before serving.

Onion, Mango <u>and</u> Peanut Chaat

Chaats are spiced relishes of vegetables and nuts served with Indian meals. Amchoor (mango powder) adds a deliciously fruity sourness to this mixture of onions and mango.

SERVES FOUR

INGREDIENTS
90g/3½oz/scant 1 cup peanuts
15ml/1 tbsp groundnut (peanut) oil
1 onion, chopped
10cm/4in piece of cucumber, seeded
   and cut into 5mm/¼in dice
1 mango, peeled, stoned (pitted)
   and diced
1 green chilli, seeded and chopped
30ml/2 tbsp chopped fresh
   coriander (cilantro)
15ml/1 tbsp chopped fresh mint
15ml/1 tbsp lime juice
pinch of soft light brown sugar
For the chaat masala
10ml/2 tsp ground cumin seeds
2.5ml/½ tsp cayenne pepper
5ml/1 tsp mango powder (amchoor)
2.5ml/½ tsp garam masala
pinch ground asafoetida
salt and ground black pepper

1 To make the chaat masala, grind all the spices together, then season with 2.5ml/½ tsp each of salt and pepper.

2 Cook the peanuts in the oil until lightly browned, then drain on kitchen paper until cool.

COOK'S TIP
Any remaining chaat masala will keep in a sealed jar for 4–6 weeks.

3 Mix the onion, cucumber, mango, chilli, fresh coriander and mint. Sprinkle in 5ml/1 tsp of the chaat masala. Stir in the peanuts and then add lime juice and/or sugar to taste. Set the mixture aside for 20–30 minutes for the flavours to mature.

4 Turn the mixture into a serving bowl, sprinkle another 5ml/1 tsp of the chaat masala over and serve.

HOT THAI PICKLED SHALLOTS

THAI PINK SHALLOTS REQUIRE LENGTHY PREPARATION, BUT THEY LOOK EXQUISITE IN THIS SPICED PICKLE. THE SHALLOTS ARE GOOD, THINLY SLICED, AS A CONDIMENT TO SOUTH-EAST ASIAN MEALS.

MAKES TWO TO THREE JARS

INGREDIENTS
    5–6 small bird's eye chillies, halved
        and seeded, if you like
    500g/1¼lb Thai pink shallots, peeled
    2 large garlic cloves, halved
For the vinegar
    600ml/1 pint/2½ cups cider vinegar
    40g/1½oz/3 tbsp granulated sugar
    10ml/2 tsp salt
    5cm/2in piece of fresh root
        ginger, sliced
    15ml/1 tbsp coriander seeds
    2 lemon grass stalks, cut in
        half lengthways
    4 kaffir lime leaves or strips of
        lime rind
    15ml/1 tbsp chopped fresh
        coriander (cilantro)

1 If leaving the chillies whole (they will be hotter if you leave the seeds in), prick them several times with a cocktail stick (toothpick). Bring a large pan of water to the boil. Blanch the chillies, shallots and garlic for 1–2 minutes, then drain. Rinse all the vegetables under cold water, then leave to drain.

2 To prepare the vinegar, put the cider vinegar, sugar, salt, ginger, coriander seeds, lemon grass and lime leaves or lime rind in a pan and bring to the boil. Simmer over a low heat for 3–4 minutes, then leave to cool.

3 Discard the ginger, then bring the vinegar back to the boil. Add the fresh coriander, garlic and chillies, and cook for 1 minute.

4 Pack the shallots into sterilized jars, distributing the lemon grass, lime leaves, chillies and garlic among them. Pour over the hot vinegar. Cool, then seal and leave in a dark place for 2 months before eating.

COOK'S TIPS
• Always be careful when making pickles to make sure that bowls and pans used for vinegar are non-reactive, that is, they are not chemically affected by the acid of the vinegar. China and glass bowls and stainless steel pans are suitable.
• When packing pickles, make sure that metal lids will not come in contact with the pickle: the acid in the vinegar will corrode the metal. Use plastic-coated or glass lids with rubber rings. Alternatively, cover the top of the jar with a round of cellophane or waxed paper to prevent direct contact when using metal lids.
• Take care when handling hot jars. Let them cool slightly after sterilizing and before filling to avoid burning yourself. However, do not let them cool completely, as they may then crack when the hot vinegar is poured in.

PICKLED MUSHROOMS WITH GARLIC AND RED ONION

THIS IS A POPULAR METHOD OF PRESERVING MUSHROOMS THROUGHOUT EUROPE. IT IS GOOD MADE WITH ONLY CULTIVATED MUSHROOMS, BUT TRY TO INCLUDE 1–2 SLICED CEPS FOR THEIR FLAVOUR.

3 Add the mushrooms and simmer for 3–4 minutes, then drain through a sieve. Retain all the herbs and spices.

4 Fill 1 large or 2 small sterilized, cooled jars with the mushrooms. Distribute the garlic, onion, herbs and spices evenly among the layers of mushrooms. Then pour in sufficient olive oil to cover by at least 1cm/½in. You may need extra oil if you use 2 jars.

5 Leave the pickle to settle, then tap the jars on the work surface to dispel any air bubbles. Seal with lids, then leave to stand for at least 2 weeks in a cool, dark place before using.

COOK'S TIP
To keep the mushrooms underneath the oil, wedge 2 wooden cocktail sticks (toothpicks) or lengths of a wooden skewer crossways in the neck of the jar.

MAKES 600ML/1 PINT/2½ CUPS

INGREDIENTS
500g/1¼lb mixed mushrooms such as small ceps, chestnut mushrooms, shiitake and girolles
300ml/½ pint/1¼ cups white wine vinegar or cider vinegar
15ml/1 tbsp sea salt
5ml/1 tsp caster (superfine) sugar
300ml/½ pint/1¼ cups water
4–5 fresh bay leaves
8 large fresh thyme sprigs
15 garlic cloves, peeled and halved, any green shoots removed
1 small red onion, halved and thinly sliced
2–3 small dried red chillies
5ml/1 tsp coriander seeds, lightly crushed
5ml/1 tsp black peppercorns
few strips of lemon rind
250–350ml/8–12fl oz/1–1½ cups extra virgin olive oil

1 Trim and wipe all the mushrooms. (It is better not to wash them, as they absorb water easily and can become waterlogged. Simply wipe them with a damp cloth or kitchen paper.) Cut large mushrooms in half.

2 Put the vinegar, salt, sugar and water in a pan and bring to the boil. Add all the remaining ingredients, apart from the mushrooms and oil. Simmer gently for 2 minutes.

CONFIT <u>of</u> SLOW-COOKED ONIONS

THIS JAM OF SLOW-COOKED, CARAMELIZED ONIONS IN SWEET-SOUR BALSAMIC VINEGAR WILL KEEP FOR SEVERAL DAYS IN A SEALED JAR IN THE REFRIGERATOR. YOU CAN USE RED, WHITE OR YELLOW ONIONS, BUT YELLOW ONIONS WILL GIVE THE SWEETEST RESULT. SHALLOTS ALSO MAKE AN EXCELLENT CONFIT.

SERVES SIX TO EIGHT

INGREDIENTS
30ml/2 tbsp olive oil
15g/½oz/1 tbsp butter
500g/1¼lb onions, sliced
3–5 fresh thyme sprigs
1 fresh bay leaf
30ml/2 tbsp light muscovado (brown)
  sugar, plus a little extra
50g/2oz/¼ cup ready-to-eat
  prunes, chopped
30ml/2 tbsp balsamic vinegar, plus
  a little extra
120ml/4fl oz/½ cup red wine
salt and ground black pepper

1 Reserve 5ml/1 tsp of the oil, then heat the rest with the butter. Add the onions, cover and cook gently for 15 minutes, stirring occasionally.

2 Season well with salt and pepper, then add the thyme, bay leaf and sugar. Cook gently, uncovered, for a further 15–20 minutes, until the onions are very soft and dark.

3 Add the prunes, vinegar and wine with 60ml/4 tbsp water and cook over a low heat, stirring frequently, for a further 20 minutes, or until most of the liquid has evaporated. Add a little water and reduce the heat if the mixture dries too quickly.

4 Adjust the seasoning, adding more sugar and/or vinegar to taste. Leave the confit to cool, then stir in the remaining 5ml/1 tsp oil. The confit is best stored for 24 hours before eating. Serve either cold or warm.

VARIATION
For Baby Onions with Tomato and Orange gently cook 500g/1¼lb peeled pickling onions or small *cipolline* in 60ml/4 tbsp olive oil until lightly browned, then sprinkle in 45ml/3 tbsp brown sugar. Let the onions caramelize a little, then add 7.5ml/1½ tsp crushed coriander seeds, 250ml/8fl oz/1 cup red wine, 2 bay leaves, a few thyme sprigs, 3 strips orange rind, 45ml/3 tbsp tomato purée (paste) and the juice of 1 orange. Cook very gently, covered, for 1 hour, stirring occasionally until the sauce is thick and reduced. Uncover for the last 20 minutes of cooking time. Sharpen with 15–30ml/ 1–2 tbsp sherry vinegar and serve cold, sprinkled with chopped parsley.

RED ONION, GARLIC AND LEMON RELISH

THIS POWERFUL RELISH IS FLAVOURED WITH NORTH-AFRICAN SPICES AND PUNCHY PRESERVED LEMONS,
AVAILABLE FROM DELICATESSENS AND LARGER SUPERMARKETS OR FROM MIDDLE-EASTERN FOOD STORES.

3 Add a pinch of salt, lots of pepper and the sugar and cook, uncovered, for 5 minutes. Soak the saffron in about 45ml/3 tbsp warm water for 5 minutes, then add to the onions, with the soaking water. Add the cinnamon stick, dried chillies, if using, and bay leaves. Stir in 30ml/2 tbsp of the sherry vinegar and the orange juice.

4 Cook over a low heat, uncovered, until the onions are very soft and most of the liquid has evaporated. Stir in the preserved lemon and cook gently for a further 5 minutes. Taste and adjust the seasoning, adding more salt, sugar and/or vinegar to taste.

5 Serve warm or cold, but not hot or chilled. The relish tastes best if it is left to stand for 24 hours.

SERVES SIX

INGREDIENTS
   45ml/3 tbsp olive oil
   3 large red onions, sliced
   2 heads of garlic, separated into
      cloves and peeled
   10ml/2 tsp coriander seeds, crushed
      but not finely ground
   10ml/2 tsp light muscovado (brown)
      sugar, plus a little extra
   pinch of saffron threads
   5cm/2in piece of cinnamon stick
   2–3 small whole dried red
      chillies (optional)
   2 fresh bay leaves
   30–45ml/2–3 tbsp sherry vinegar
   juice of ½ small orange
   30ml/2 tbsp chopped
      preserved lemon
   salt and ground black pepper

1 Heat the oil in a heavy pan. Add the onions and stir, then cover and reduce the heat to the lowest setting. Cook for 10–15 minutes, stirring occasionally, until the onions are soft.

2 Add the garlic cloves and coriander seeds. Cover and cook for 5–8 minutes, until the garlic is soft.

VARIATION
To make a quick Lebanese onion relish, chop 500g/1¼lb ripe tomatoes and combine with 1 bunch of sliced spring onions (scallions) or 4–6 small grelots. Crush 2 cloves of garlic with a large pinch of salt and gradually work in 15ml/1 tbsp lemon juice and 45–60ml/ 3–4 tbsp extra virgin olive oil. Toss the tomatoes and onions with the dressing and stir in a small bunch of chopped purslane or 30ml/2 tbsp chopped marjoram or lemon thyme, then adjust the seasoning with salt, pepper, a pinch of sugar and maybe more lemon juice. Serve with lamb or chicken or a bulgur wheat salad or couscous.

INDEX